Creating With the Angels

An Angel-Guided Journey Into Creativity

Other Books
by Terry Lynn Taylor

**Messengers of Light:
The Angels' Guide to Spiritual Growth**

**Guardians of Hope:
The Angels' Guide to Personal Growth**

**Answers From the Angels:
A Book of Angel Letters**

Creating With the Angels

An Angel-Guided Journey Into Creativity

Terry Lynn Taylor

H J Kramer Inc
Tiburon, California

H J Kramer Inc
P.O. Box 1082
Tiburon, CA 94920

Editor: Nancy Grimley Carleton
Illustrations: Marty Noble
Cover Art: Rosso Fiorentino, 15th century, Italian, Angel With Lute
Cover Design: Jim Marin-Pixel Media
Composition: Classic Typography
Book Production: Schuettge and Carleton
Manufactured in the United States of America.
10 9 8 7 6 5 4 3 2 1

Fiorentino painting:
Courtesy of Superstock

Library of Congress Cataloging-in-Publication Data

Taylor, Terry Lynn, 1955–
Creating with the angels : an angel-guided journey into creativity / Terry Lynn Taylor.
p. cm.
Includes bibliographical references.
ISBN 0-915811-49-9 : $9.95
1. Angels–Miscellanea. 2. Creative ability–Miscellanea.
3. Creation (Literary, artistic, etc.)–Miscellanea. I. Title.
BL477.T375 1993 93–33186
291.2′15–dc20 CIP

Dedication

The angels would like you to know:

Creativity

Creativity is very special.
You are born with lots of it.
As you get older, you get more and
more creative, because you know more
about everything than when you were a baby.
With creativity, you can make whatever you
want. It doesn't matter what the things
you make look like, because we're
all different and creative
in different ways.
Elizabeth Ann Godfrey, age twelve

To Our Readers

The books we publish are our contribution to an emerging world based on cooperation rather than on competition, on affirmation of the human spirit rather than on self-doubt, and on the certainty that all humanity is connected. Our goal is to touch as many lives as possible with a message of hope for a better world.

Hal and Linda Kramer, Publishers

Contents

Contents

Foreword

One of the most essential areas of our life on earth and our impact on the heavens above is the ability of humanity to expand creativity. To work fully with creativity means cooperating with the angels of God, and thus it is fitting that Terry Taylor has chosen this topic to enhance a wonderful body of work that includes *Messengers of Light, Guardians of Hope,* and *Answers From the Angels.*

What makes *Creating With the Angels* and Terry's other work unique is not only that she writes in a way that inspires us to rejoice in an awareness of the angels but also that her work originates from a spirit and soul that truly honors the Greatest Creator of all. I believe Terry has let a stream of purity flow through her work that reflects her sincere intentions to be of real and lasting service to the realms of heaven.

When I first met Terry, I was struck with the similarity she bears to some of the classical paintings of the archangel Raphael. It is interesting to note that she especially loves Raphael, and his love for her shines out in her work and in her desire to ease suffering through an awareness of the joy the angels can bring to us.

This book is essential for our time; it offers a guidepost for increasing our creative abilities in a way that contributes to the world in which we live. And perhaps through these pages many will be inspired to dwell more completely in the consciousness of the Divine Creator.

K. Martin-Kuri

Introduction:

This Is Your Creative Wake-up Call From the Angels!

One of the important things to remember is that the way we attract angels is by becoming the qualities that are of interest to them. When we focus on such qualities as compassion, faith, or tolerance, we attract angelic beings that are trying to help develop that in all humanity.
K. Martin-Kuri

Angels act as messengers of God. They communicate with us through inspiration. When we fill our everyday lives with spiritual essence and ask the angels to join us, we create angel consciousness. Angel consciousness entails more than just focusing on the wonder of angels; its scope includes noticing the wonder of God everywhere and in everything and sharing and cocreating this wonder with the angels. Angel consciousness helps us keep heavenly qualities alive right here on earth. We not only *see* the beauty around us; we *feel* it in our soul. We don't merely *hear* celestial music; our beings *resonate* to it. Angels, as messengers of heaven, help us make life a true and meaningful experience. This in turn allows us to raise the vibration of love on planet earth. If you want to be a part of expanding the light of love on earth right now, a good and a fun way to start is by filling your consciousness with angels.

Oftentimes, when people first start to increase their angel consciousness, their whole perception of life changes. People feel very happy when they find out that they can focus on something that is solely positive in nature. When we reawaken our awareness of angels and bring angel consciousness into our everyday lives, something shifts. We notice that a force "bigger than us" is at play in our lives for the highest good of all. We see, sense, hear, feel, know, and enjoy positive results.

When the angels become a positive focus in our lives, we feel a deep urge to express ourselves creatively. Our creative expression doesn't necessarily entail painting a picture or doing a craft; it means that the angels inspire us to allow our innate creative energy to flow in every arena, so that our lives themselves become beautiful creations. The angels teach us that creativity is a natural way of life. We are creative every day whether we realize it or not. As my editor, Nancy Grimley Carleton, so aptly put it, "We're all blessed with creative energy, and our creativity can be expressed through painting a picture, writing a book, planting a garden, preparing a wonderful dinner for family or friends, creating a loving environment for animals, nurturing a child, creating community and relationships, and countless other ways."

Our innate creativity is reawakened and intensified by the angels, because the angels are totally creative in everything they do—in the ways they communicate with us, in the ways they inspire us, and in the ways they protect us. The angels are like a big flow of creative energy, and this energy always surrounds us like a gentle pressure, a comfortable wind, or a creative force waiting to come through and inspire us in special ways. Stop for a moment and imagine the loving, creative energy that the angels are always moving your way. Begin to allow it to awaken fully in your own life. Each time you allow this flow of creative energy—angel energy—to stream through your being, you expand this energy and you can soar to great heights.

The angelic reinforcement of personal creativity pleases me more than any other angelic influence. When I noticed how the angels were helping so many people to unleash their creativity, I felt the desire to help spur the momentum in whatever way I could. So I offer this book in the hope that it will help to inspire you to expand your own special form of creativity in cooperation with the angels. Creativity is not really something you can learn from a book; it is an awakening—a process. My main objective is to help you dislodge outmoded beliefs about creativity and open to the message from the angels that it is crucial for you to express your creativity.

Just the word *creativity* can evoke amazing reactions in people. For those who think they are not creative, it may bring up feelings of longing. For others who have left their creativity alone for too long, yet know in their hearts that they are creative, the word may uncover feelings of jealousy and even anger. People who are actively living their creativity may resonate with joy when they hear the word. How do you react when you think of your own creativity? Your reaction may indicate whether you are truly flowing with your creative energy or whether something is blocking it. When you create with the angels and bring the angels into your everyday life, your feelings about creativity naturally expand. Without a lot of fanfare, you will wake up one day and realize that each breath you take represents a stream of creative energy. Creative energy is all around you, and so are the angels.

The angels help us express what is inside of us. They help us peel off the outside layers to reveal our youthful spirit of creative energy. The outside layers of an onion are dry and tough because they serve to protect the onion. Your outside layers may be dry and tough because they serve to protect your sacred creativity, which is vulnerable and alive with spirit. The angels can offer you a different kind of protection so that you no longer need to hide your spirit under layers of pain and confusion.

As you read this book, keep a running thought in the back of your mind, such as "I am a creative being, inspired by the angels, full of exciting ideas and boundless creative energy." Even if you don't fully believe this affirmation, keep it or another positive affirmation about yourself as a creative being in your mind as often as you can. Be on constant alert for, and open to, the creative ways the angels send you messages. You may need to set the book down while reading and run with the creative inspiration that the angels send you. Go for it; follow the angelic creativity moving you to action. If you do, your soul will delight, your spirit will sing, your body will enjoy, your mind will lighten up, and your whole life will serve as a creative statement.

On a more serious note (if you're familiar with my philosophy, you know that I rarely use the word *serious*; I use it now because I'm about to tell you my "bottom line," my code, my raison d'être): The core purpose behind our existence is to create. When I start to ponder the "whys" of life and try to understand such things as the suffering in the world, the injustice, the mysterious reason for our being here, sometimes I get to a point where I can't imagine why we should even bother and I feel depressed. When this happens, I know I had better stop these thoughts and immediately begin to create with the angels.

At such moments, I take some time to write, cook, tend my garden, or sketch in my journal. It doesn't matter which; what matters is that I create. When I change my direction and use my energy to create with the angels, life makes sense again. I feel my inner happiness glowing brightly once more, thanks to my choice to create with the angels.

If heaven turns out to be a place where all we do is create, that will be fine with me. God is the ultimate Creator, so heaven has got to be a very creative place. To bring heaven to earth, all we have to do is recognize the creative energy that exists all around us and use it to express ourselves and to make positive, heavenly gains in the here and now. If you ask me why we are here on earth, I would have to answer: to expand our creativity, to create in our own unique ways, to express ourselves and our love, and to keep the creative flame alive and burning brightly within our hearts. Don't let the flame—the vital creative energy force—dim or go out. No matter how dark the world seems, no matter how depressing life gets, heaven's light is always available. Keep your life force strong by creating with the angels!

About the Structure of the Book

My goal in presenting the information in this book is to give you a creative experience even while you're reading. I want to stir up your creative energy in new ways and urge you to "make creative choices with the angels," to start tuning into what is most important for you to do in each moment. With the angels, you will be able to adopt fresh perspectives and experience a new openness to explore all possibilities. Through playfulness and imagination, the angels will guide you in creating an artistic response to life. The most creative thing you can ever do as a human is to be fully alive and present in the here and now. When you achieve full mindfulness of the moment, you are in full harmony with the creative flow.

I did something rather silly the other day. I asked my five-year-old neighbor, Oriann, if she knew what creativity was. She looked at me a bit strangely and replied, "No," but said that if I wanted to explain the word I could. Well, how do you explain the word *creativity* to a five-year-old? I found myself stumbling for words and finally said, "Well, it means doing things like drawing, dancing, art, writing, and playing." A very sweet smile spread over Oriann's face, and she said, "Oh, so there is a word for all of that." Once again, I am faced with the limitations of words, but words can point us toward inner truth. It is not the words themselves but the life behind them with which I am most concerned. Hopefully, while you are reading this book, the angels will join you and take you behind the scenes, where the words fade out and being at one with the moment is all that matters.

Part One of this book is about harvesting angelic inspiration. I approached this part with a sense of spontaneity and play, two extremely important components to the creative process. I started by thinking about qualities and states of being that the angels would want us to create in our everyday lives. The two inspiring elements behind all of the ideas I put forth in Part One are personal freedom and spiritual integrity. Freedom, when cultivated, allows us to be ourselves. Integrity is being true to ourselves. While this definition of integrity has almost become cliché, it is nevertheless essential that we keep on the path of true self-expression. You came into this life to be yourself, not someone else, and the sooner you are true to yourself, the sooner you will accomplish and enjoy what you really came here for. In Part One, you will find a selection of ideas to help to free the creative spirit. Feel free to modify the ideas or expand upon them in whatever way fits your own angelic inspiration. I approached all of the ideas with the sense of the angels nearby. Sometimes I felt them looking over my shoulder as I wrote; other times, I was reading or doing something else, and they would bring me a creative idea and I would run to the computer to write. Most of all, while I wrote this section, I felt myself becoming a freer spirit. When this book is finished, by the time you are reading it, I will be treating myself to some new paints and a bag of clay. I will be taking voice lessons and dancing whenever I can. I'll be going on long walks and studying clouds. I will revel in the sunsets and moonrises. And I vow to be available to play at the drop of a hat!

As sometimes happens in human life, we occasionally reach a point where we must remove the blocks before traveling any further. The blocks that impede our creative spirit exist only in our minds. Since the mind is part of the vehicle for our creative self-expression, it is important to resolve or remove these blocks when they are having a real effect on us. Part Two of this book offers some ideas for releasing the blocks and expressing your highest self. Life on earth does get a bit muddy at times, especially after it rains. Mud can actually be fun for a while. I used to love to play in the mud as a child. My friends and I would have contests to see who could get the most covered with mud. I often won the contest. The great thing about mud is that it comes off so easily—just a little water and, presto, we're clean again. The mud that cakes on our "wings" and weighs our spirits down requires spiritual water to remove it. This spiritual cleansing can take place almost as easily as getting rid of earth mud, but the process is a little more difficult to see, because we have to use our hearts to feel and our mind's eyes to see where the mud is hiding. Once we "see" it and become aware of it, we can make the conscious choice to get rid of it. The best way to tackle mud is not to take it too seriously, to have some fun. So approach the ideas in this part of the book as just another game to play, one in which everyone wins.

Part Three of this book consists of three journeys I wrote with the intention of teaching from a different perspective. The journeys are designed either to be read or to be used as guided meditations. They focus on self-love. Self-love is our ultimate lesson and absolutely essential for creativity to flourish, so I wanted to offer a range of experiences to get this message across.

In Part Four, I asked some people I know who have made the choice to live creative lives to share some of their experiences with creativity and the way the angels influence them. Again, the spirit of the angels pervaded; all of the contributors wanted to share their experiences so that others might be inspired to open more fully to the angels and their own innate creativity. We are all teachers for one another. Sometimes we don't even realize what we are truly teaching. If we live our lives with integrity and trust, our teachings will raise the vibrations of love on the planet.

Think of this book as a soul-help book instead of a self-help book. The angels love you!

Part One
Creating With the Angels

About Part One

> *. . . I came to understand that what motivated these men was not Earthly prizes or the respect of colleagues, but that they put their souls and minds on something and reached the extraordinary place where the mind could no longer produce data of the type that they wanted, and they were in the territory of inspiration where their intuitions accelerated and they knew that there was something more than the realm of time and space and matter, something more than physical life. They knew it.*
>
> Gary Zukav, referring to William James, Carl Jung, Benjamin Lee Whorf, Niels Bohr, and Albert Einstein, *Seat of the Soul*

The ideas presented in this section are meant to help you set yourself creatively free through angelic inspiration. We all know too well the feeling of being uninspired; the angels want to make sure you can bypass this feeling in the future of your creative spirit by learning to access the angelic realm for pure inspiration. Inspiration is how the angels guide and teach us. Inspiration stirs the fire in our souls. To create anything wonderful, we must first be inspired; inspiration is the most important component of greatness. We all have it in us, and the angels know exactly what to inspire in us. They inspirit our beings with divine light, offering a direct transmission from God. The angels can inspire you to give love to the world in your own special way, to live a creative life in harmony with the divine cosmic dance, and to create a noble life-style. Angelic inspiration comes to you when you play and cultivate spontaneity. Creative impulses come when you are fully alive and willing to get carried away on a wing and a prayer. When all is said and done, the angels inspire you to have a good laugh and lighten up.

Allow this section of the book to be fun for you, to bring you closer to the angels, and to provide creative feelings. I picked ideas I felt that the angels wanted to help all of us develop. Ultimately, the angels want to instill in us the courage to think freely and stand up for ourselves as creative beings. The angels are there to help us stand tall and creative. In order to create the courage to live your creativity, always think for yourself. Seek questions to ask, but ask the questions of yourself. By this, I mean search for the answers in your own soul, in your own intuition, from your own guides; using whatever form works for you, start to look within for answers. Most of us ask questions of others that only we can truly answer. All of the answers are right in front of our noses, waiting to be discovered. If you have the question, you have the answer. Your angels know what you are looking for. When the angels help you find your answers, they have very creative ways of guiding you. So the more creative you allow yourself to be, the more in tune with the angels' messages you will be.

Creating essential qualities the angels are interested in can help you fertilize the soil for creative germination; this process will allow your creative expression to be complete, high, light, and purely you. Each time you start a creative endeavor, think about ways the angels can encourage you and help you with it. Read the ideas in this section, then expand them with your own creativity. My true desire with this book is to offer inspiration that may encourage you to create a beautiful and creative life with the angels so that you can express your being to the world in your own unique way. The angels love you and know the secrets of your soul. They know you are creative, and they hold a vision of your finest creative qualities at all times. The angels are with you on each creative journey you undertake – not only to give you a glimpse of the divine but also to give you a deeper experience of here-and-now reality.

Most of all, the angels want to encourage you to have fun, be wild, laugh, frolic, play, be courageous, and create spontaneity. The angels are right here right now, waiting to have some fun with you. Look up and give them an affirmative nod to let them know you acknowledge their loving presence.

Chapter 1
Personal Freedom

God made us angels of energy, encased in solids—currents of life dazzling through a material bulb of flesh.
Paramahansa Yogananda

In this chapter I was inspired to write about creating ideas that allow us to see life in our own ways and create meaningful, deep experiences of living it. These ideas don't entail a lonely path, marching to a different drummer—not anymore—because there are many of us wanting to live with personal freedom and we will always find one another. We will be able to enrich one another through our creative living. The angels are attracted to free spirits who aren't afraid of being themselves, even if the bulk of society can't seem to understand them. The angels always understand us when we are real. When we play with the angels, we learn something new and exciting each day. The world is fresh with wonder and meaning, and we know that no matter where we are, or what situation we are in, our minds are free to create with the angels.

When we want to live a creative life with the angels, we need to build a new structure for our lives based on personal freedom. Personal freedom gives us the chance to be who we really want to be—ourselves—and the courage not to give into others' beliefs and ways of doing things when they don't fit our creative system. For personal freedom to flourish and generate creative impulses, the following ideas help:

- Be willing to drop rigid beliefs.
- Give up harsh judgments about fellow humans. Don't be ruled by judgments.
- Change your mind whenever you please; think, question, and philosophize.
- Realize how impressive peace is.
- Do not run on a strict time schedule; slow down, and allow room for something interesting to develop.
- Have a flexible mind and body.
- Make an ass out of yourself once in a while; it can do you good.
- Never "live down" to anyone's expectations.
- Be a good friend to yourself.
- Be authentic.
- Dare to be humorous; dare to be yourself.
- Allow space for imperfection in yourself and others; our imperfections make us interesting.
- Let go of your gripes; surrender your stubborn ways.
- Don't let yourself think or feel that you are at the mercy of the world; God's angels are guarding you night and day.
- Give up any defensive attitude you may carry around; it is okay to make mistakes or to be "wrong."
- Pay attention to your gut feelings.
- Try something new often.
- Breathe deeply at least once an hour, and let yourself feel enthusiastic.
- Know you deserve the best the angels have to offer.

- Explore, experiment, enjoy things, expect the unexpected, leave a window open for spirit, shout from rooftops, be a Spanish dancer, cultivate laughing attacks, and think of something wild to do each day, and you will keep your guardian angel well entertained and happy.
- Let freedom ring!

Creating Success

I run into people all the time who are paralyzed
by the fact that they might fail.
To me, there's no failure. This is all an exploration.
John Sayles

Who decides what makes some things successes and others failures? Are there really any failures? Calling something a failure is a judgment we make, usually based on comparisons. There is no true comparison to you; you are an original and everything you do is successful if you choose to see it that way.

When my younger sister was five years old, she cut her bangs to about a quarter inch the very day she was going to have her class picture taken. I walked into the room just as she had completed this act and asked her, "What on earth are you doing?" She answered, "I'm doing an experiment." I'll never forget those words. Of course, her experiment was not one of my mother's favorites, but the incident became a family classic and ripe with humor. Learn to experiment and not judge the outcome as a success or failure. Rather, look at your experiment in terms of what you have learned and the fun you had in the process. Experiments may not always "succeed" the way we want them to, but we have the choice to focus on the value of what we've learned.

One way to choose success is to figure out what your values are—the things in your life that are the most important to you personally. When I worked with children in a human relations program, we would ask them to list their values, after we explained what values were. About 90 percent of the time, the top value on their lists was family. I found that wonderful. Other values high on their lists were love, education, pets, friends, home, school, community, hope, peace, and religion. Make a list of your values. When you want to know if you are a success or not, look at your values and ask yourself if you have compromised them in any way. Compromising your values means you have not been true to yourself; you have created a rift in your consciousness. Sometimes we take the easy way out—or what we view as the easy way—to achieve money or success. The easy way often goes against our values and against the highest good for all. Think about the times you have felt like a failure and see if you're acting against your values. When you find yourself feeling like a failure, forgive yourself and then concentrate on changing what you're doing to bring yourself into alignment with your values for the highest good of all concerned.

When we think of success, too often we put a monetary and worldly measure on it. This can cause us to compromise or to remove ourselves from that which is truly meaningful to us. Workaholics and people who are obsessed with climbing the ladder of success usually come to a turning point where they reassess, evaluate their values, and change their course to a simpler and more meaningful way of life. In terms of your own creativity, learn to follow through with your commitments simply because by doing so you express who you truly are, not because it may bring money, fame, and so forth. A quotation that has stayed in my mind for years is one from Uta Hagen, a famous acting teacher. She said, "Love the art in yourself, not yourself in the art." In my own life, loving the art in myself has been a true source of joy. When you love the art in yourself, you are loving the divine Creator, and your success is measured by divine bliss and abundant gifts.

The Angels Know You Are Successful

1. Start to think of success in terms of your own values, and you will never fail. You will explore and educate yourself. In fact, maybe we should redefine the word *success* and allow ourselves to be free to live according to our own highest standards and values.

2. List some new ways you can view success in your everyday life.

3. List ways you feel the angels view success.

4. Take a stand. Find out what you have to say, and say it. Think of what you stand for. Is it true? Do you know what you stand for? If you don't, and you want to make your mark on the world, you'd better find out what you stand for and be willing to act accordingly. By this, I don't mean fighting for your opinions. You have something inside you that is waiting to be said, and the angels can help you say it. Taking a stand involves reexamining your values and asking yourself: Do I stand for my values? True success entails finding out who you are and becoming comfortable with who you are. The more you know about yourself, the more you will know how to live in accordance

with your values. You will have your own unique way of doing this, and it will bring you grace and inner happiness—true success. Leave room for growth and expansion.

5. Make a list of your current truths. Many of our truths lie hidden, yet they have powerful effects on our life-style. The following is a sampling of a few of the truths that I find swimming around in my consciousness at the present moment. The funny thing is that these truths may change. By the time you are reading them, they may no longer be my truths, but this is just the nature of truth and another reminder not to take ourselves too seriously. My truths now include:

- There is a spiritual answer to each psychological or physical problem.
- God is love.
- Life is strange and wonder-full.
- We are here for a creative reason.
- Our imagination is a place of truth and beauty.
- This list will never end, and I'll always be discovering yet another truth.

Creating Your Space

It's so important to unclutter the mind. For me,
creativity is greatly impeded just by the chatter
and visual clutter of life. It's really important
to have a space that is really clear
for whatever is emerging to come.
Alice Walker

Sometimes when I sit down and attempt to write something or do something creative, I feel guilty—as if I don't have the time or I should be taking care of business. Worries and thoughts about other people start to interfere, and eventually I get sidetracked and end up not writing very much. One way around this is to create "sacred space." When you feel a worry or thought intrude into your sacred space, tell the outside interference that it must leave *now*—this is time for creativity. All of the seemingly pressing issues can wait to be dealt with after this designated time. When you are in sacred space, you will thrive when you follow these guidelines:

- No worrying.
- No stewing.
- No pondering over the world's troubles.
- No focusing on physical pain.
- No answering the phone.
- No television on in the background
- No guilt feelings allowed.

Another way to be aware of sacred space is by allowing the space where you live to resonate with your essence. Even if you are living somewhere temporary (who isn't?), you can make your living space your own and express parts of yourself that you like to be reminded of. Many people collect angel figurines and other angel-related material. Having reminders of the angels around can help you keep your focus on the divine help and light that are always available to you.

Space Available

1. Create a bubble of protection with the angels. When you need sacred space, ask the angels to help you visualize

a protective bubble of light around you. The angels will fly around the perimeter of this bubble and ward off any negative influences that would otherwise interfere with your creative energy. They may even intercept phone calls or visits until you are available.

2. Always remember that you have an inner sanctum, a holy place, within you that you need to protect. This inner room is not just a place for your mind; it is a sacred private place where your whole being resides. To keep it pure and full of energy, you can cocreate protection with your guardian angel. If something doesn't feel right, keep it away. Some people have so intimately developed their inner sanctum that the minute they feel uncomfortable, they don't wait for their minds to explain it (which may come too late); rather, they allow their gut feelings to guide them far away. I know some people who get sick to their stomachs when they sense negative energy; sometimes they don't believe their gut feelings, but later the truth supports their initial reactions. Be aware and ask that your guardian angel help you keep your inner sanctum safe and sound. Then follow through with the guidance. Don't look back.

3. Protect your solar plexus, located at your gut. Sensitive individuals may think that most of the negative input they find difficult to handle comes in through their own minds, but the most damaging input actually comes in through the solar plexus. Sensitive people usually have very aware and acutely developed minds. So they intellectually know and sense when something isn't right; the trouble is, they sometimes forget to protect their solar plexus. When you have a sense that something isn't right or that there is something "dark" nearby, ask your angels to help you flood light out through your solar plexus for protection. Or

visualize the angels helping you put on a "light" suit of armor to protect you.

Creating the Unconventional

Creativity can replace conformity as the primary mode of social being. We can cling to that which is passing, or has already passed, or we can remain accessible to—even surrender to—the creative process, without insisting that we know in advance the ultimate outcome for us, our institutions, or our planet.
Stephen Nachmanovitch,
Free Play: Improvisation in Life and Art

Although I enjoy certain customs, rituals, and ceremonies, I passionately believe that it is important for us to be a bit unconventional. By this, I don't mean being unconventional to the point where we annoy others or attack their beliefs; such aggression serves no one. *Unconventional* means not bound by custom or convention and denotes the unusual. Being unconventional is important is because it fosters personal freedom of expression. Also, it can help us find new ways to present ideas and discover different ways of doing the same thing that might more truly reflect our style. This idea of being unconventional may be a bit scary to some people if they feel they don't live in a supportive environment. I grew up in a conservative town, and anything unusual was of great curiosity. Any indication that a neighbor might be eccentric elicited everyone's interest. Once an art teacher I know, in this same conservative town, painted her front door bright orange, and the neighbors became quite upset. If an orange door was all they had to worry about, they should have gone and kissed that door! Often we have to be brave and take a stand when we want to express ourselves.

Unconventional Expression

1. I have heard it said that the reason so many "wild" people live in California is that all of the pioneers and innovators who wanted more freedom moved west, away from conventional, conservative towns. I'm not so sure I believe this, having grown up in California, but I have found that many people definitely did go west to find a sense of freedom. If you are feeling painfully repressed because of where you live, you might want to consider moving. If you are feeling repressed but love where you live, find ways to be yourself gently. The world is forever changing, and we can help the change along by living our creativity and expressing who we are regardless of whether this fits in with others' expectations. Take "baby steps," doing little unconventional things that may go unnoticed at first, and then build up to larger announcements. Some people may even think that those of us who know the angels are unconventional by the very nature of our believing in and knowing something that is supernatural.

2. Forget the issue of being popular. Who really cares if others "like" you as long as you love yourself and have a few good friends and allies? If you are not being yourself, people don't really like *you* anyway. Be aware of why change and being unconventional can be difficult, but hold this thought lightly. Change is usually difficult because we are afraid of rocking the boat. Go ahead! Jump up and down in the boat, but

make sure you have a life jacket (the angels) with you if you fall out.

3. I have always thought that more people should hang flags and banners in the front of their houses for special and unusual occasions. This is a great way to be creative, especially if you design and sew the flag yourself. It is also a way to be unconventional, because your flag could call people's attention to something thought provoking and positive, like the angels.

4. Good luck! Remember to let your unconventional ploys out a little at a time and subtly send the message that you are not completely bound by custom or convention.

Creating the Unexpected

Expectations and belief are the sculptors of reality. Whatever we expect will be our experience. If we expect recovery to be hard, painful, and lifelong, that is what life will give us. If we learn to still our expectations, we will be constantly amazed at life's gifts.
Joseph V. Bailey, *The Serenity Principle*

Do you ever feel as if you have to explain everything you do to some anonymous or named person who may be watching? Sometimes I feel this way because I often find myself doing the unexpected, based on the reactions I get. People often ask me "why" questions–Why did you put that there? Why are you reading that? Why did you park that way? Apparently these questions arise because I didn't do what they expected. As we all know, people often become uncomfortable when their expectations are not met. We can allow others' reactions of discomfort to trap and bind our creative freedom when we think too much about what others might think or expect, or when we get too attached to our own expectations.

Sometimes when I am writing, I start to go in a certain direction or use a certain word because I think that's what others would expect. As soon as I am aware I'm following an expectation, I change directions and go with what I really want to say and do. The bottom line is I have to be true to myself. Too often we try to project logic onto all that we do, and logic is really just a process of talking to ourselves, trying to make sense out of that vital force called life. Why bother? Just express.

Start to be aware in your own life when you start to behave a certain way because someone else may expect it and you are trying to avoid being questioned about your behavior. Someone wise once said, "I refuse to live down to anyone's expectations." Refuse to "live down" to others' expectations. We offer a good lesson to everyone when we do the unexpected. Of course, I would never suggest doing the unexpected just to shake others up or shock them. All we need to do is to be true to ourselves.

Express, Don't Expect!

1. Expectation traps include straight lines, acceptable colors, manicured lawns, "normal" behavior, right use of language, concepts of right and wrong, and so forth. Think of some of the potential traps you notice in your own life.

2. The angels never expect you to be anything other than a being of love. The angels will let you know that when you cease expecting, you gain all things.

3. Remember that you don't have to explain yourself to anyone. When we express ourselves in a way others don't understand, they may try to impose their beliefs on us so that we will admit that we "should" have done something different. There is no such thing as "should." Go ahead and do the unexpected and expect the unexpected. Express yourself. If you are questioned, you can always quote Fritz Perls:

I do my thing, and you do your thing.
I am not in this world to live up to your expectations,
And you are not in this world to live up to mine.
You are you, and I am I,
And if by chance, we find each other, it's beautiful.
If not, it can't be helped.

Creating Privacy

The desire for privacy is not a precious adolescent attitude,
but an essential element of nurture and protection.
Kay Leigh Hagan, *Internal Affairs*

It is okay to create privacy. This means you can have private thoughts that no one else ever needs to know or hear, private activities that only you know about, and private feelings you want to keep inside. Even if you want to have a private life-style that you share with only a few people—this is all okay! I used to think that I was not supposed to keep anything to myself, including thoughts, feelings, or activities I was pursuing. When I kept them to myself, I felt guilty and uncomfortable about doing so. I guess I thought that honesty meant being candid all of the time about everything. Then I realized that it was okay to be a private person. I gave myself permission to choose who needs to know what and when. Some people have grown up in environments where they had no privacy, and now they either become too private–almost isolated and secluded–or they simply don't know how to create the privacy they need in their adult life or don't think it is okay to create it.

Think about your own issues of privacy and how you can create a level of privacy that feels appropriate in your own life. It is up to you to decide how personal you want to be with someone. There are different levels of relating within each friendship, and each friendship or relationship you have is unique. You have a right to protect your own mental health. If you want to keep things from people, that is your business; you are not violating anyone's right to know, because there is no such thing. There are no rules in the universe that say in order to be a good friend and a good person you have to live a totally open life, available to spill your guts to whomever might come along.

The Angels Respect Your Privacy

1. Your creativity offers a wonderful arena for expressing private thoughts, feelings, or experiences. You can paint a picture with a certain meaning, and no one needs to know except you. You can write a cryptic poem. You can write a novel based on characters that represent a private aspect of yourself. You can write your feelings in your journal using a secret code, or you can write about yourself in the third person, using a secret code name.

2. Imagine that the angels are in on your secrets. Share your private thoughts with the angels. The angels are your private cheering section, cheering for your highest good, and sometimes being private is for your highest good.

3. If someone asks you a direct question about something private and you don't want to answer, ask yourself, "Does this person really need to know that?" You are the judge when you are asked something personal. Ask the angels to help you; they can actually create a barrier to protect your privacy. If you feel that someone is invading or about to invade your privacy, ask the angels to change the subject for you. Feel protected; the angels respect your privacy. One way to deflect an invading question is to repeat the question as a statement back to the person asking; then politely say you are not comfortable answering the question at this time.

Creating Enjoyment

Not only is practice necessary to art, it is art.
Stephen Nachmanovitch, *Free Play*

To experience true pleasure from your own deep and mysterious creativity, you have to persist. One creative encounter is not going to do it. This means you must practice. By practice, I don't mean creating forced, regimented, strict, or disciplined time when you stress yourself trying to learn something or where you drill yourself until you can't take it anymore. I mean having ongoing fun with your creativity and making practice an exploration of joy and fun. By practicing with a sense of fun and exploration, you create a special time where you can play with new colors in your paintings, listen to a type of music you would normally avoid, throw clay on the walls and floors, or even write swear words in your journal. In other words, turn practice time into more than going over the "same old stuff." Practicing in this manner will help you to free the muse and discover hidden creativity that you might otherwise miss.

Practice does not make "perfect," because here on earth there is no such thing. But practice can bring a sense of greatness to your creativity and give you courage. With practice, you can become more "at one" with your art, more nonthinking–oriented more toward doing and being. If you are not enjoying yourself when you practice, stop and figure out why. We have enough stress and "shoulds" in our lives, and we don't need to bring these problems into our creative time.

Practicing Angel Joy

1. Think of new ways to practice your creativity. Perhaps you can gain more insight into one form of art or creativity by practicing one you are not familiar with and then transferring what you've learned to the form you are already familiar with. Play, explore, and enjoy practicing. It is an integral part of life, so make it fun.

2. Practice with the angels as your special teachers. Play with what you're creating, and then stop and receive their wisdom. Ask them how to enjoy your practice even more!

Creating Celebration

A celebration is a sharing of common memory and, therefore, a forgetting of private memory. All

become one again. The past is present; the present past; the future forgotten yet here: this is the way God thinks on time. God, after all, is oblivious of the future, yet present fully to all times.
Matthew Fox, *Whee! We, Wee All the Way Home*

To celebrate means to honor an event with festivities, to "make merry," and to show that a day or event is important. We celebrate on obvious holidays, but sometimes it is fun to find something new and obscure to celebrate. Many people can express their creativity in this way. Think of something out of the blue and celebrate it. For example, what if the word *onion* comes into your mind? How could you celebrate onions? Easy: Make onion soup, serve it with onion bread, find some unique information about onions, and pass the information on to whomever you talk with that day. Paint a picture of an onion, learn to juggle with onions, play catch with an onion, go to a nursery and find some onion plants, and so forth. There are so many ways to celebrate, and once you develop a "celebration mind-set," you will find the world is full of possibilities for joyful celebration.

Go Celebrate!

1. Here are a few celebration ideas: Celebrate yourself, your favorite color, rainbows, a tree beginning to bud, cats, the sun and moon, your favorite food, or a favorite poet or writer. And, of course, there are many ways to celebrate the angels!

2. Make a shrine to honor your celebration theme. Dress accordingly. Take off with the angels and celebrate life!

3. Entertainment means "to amuse, to occupy agreeably,

to create amusement, and to receive a person with hospitality." To entertain an idea means to have it in your mind. Entertain the idea that life is amusing. Consider the possibility of celebrating with the angels all the special moments of each day. Have you entertained your angels lately?

Creating the Dance

For those of you whose take on the world is more kinesthetic than imaginative, the dance is critical and often leads to a sudden realization of deeper implications.
Jean Houston

The dance of life is more than just a physical movement or rhythm. The dance is a metaphor for spiritual living and relationships. If you see yourself dancing through life, you will know that sometimes you are dancing by yourself, with only the angels joining you. At other times, you are dancing in a group, and your movements depend on the group mind. Other times, you may engage in an intimate dance with a special partner. The dance of life can be slow, fast, lively, solemn, silent, loud, giving, taking; it is spiritual movement of the soul, spirit, and body.

Dance to the beat of your own special music. Join the cosmic dance of the universe. Think of the world's various cultures; each one has at least one special dance. Think of the freedom that dancing brings your soul. Dancing can be a way of praising the Creator. Appreciate dancing whenever you see it. Remember that the angels are dancing around in your consciousness, waking your soul up to the creative life force all around you.

Waltzing on the Threshold

1. Rent a Fred Astaire movie or an old musical, or take ballroom dancing lessons. Watch folk dancing, or take a class to learn folk dancing. Think of all of the various types of dance classes offered. If you decide to take one, bring the angels with you as invisible dance partners.

2. One very special form of dancing, which my friend Shannon and I have been practicing for years, is living room dancing. Put on your favorite music and dance by yourself in the privacy of your living room. Invite the angels to join you.

3. Watch your own dance of life and ask yourself if you need some added bounce in your step. If you do, be creative and introduce some new moves into your daily dance with life.

Creating Originality

Every creative act involves a new innocence of perception, liberated from the cataract of accepted belief.
Arthur Koestler

I've heard it said that there are no new ideas. If you come up with an idea that you think is original, someone somewhere has probably had the same idea or will soon. Many ideas are intentionally copied, sometimes edging out the artists who first presented the ideas. There are idea wolves in the world and people who think they can take someone's creativity and make it better, but don't let this stop you from striving to be original. Never give up; if you continue to grow and live creatively, you will come out a winner.

Within the word *original* is the word *origin*. What is the origin of creativity? Who started all of this? Where do ideas really come from? Think about these questions, and look for your own answers. Remember that communicating with words can be limiting. How can words really express a mystery? How can they express the deepest spiritual truths? Please don't get hung up on words and concepts; play with them, and take them lightly.

The *Oxford American Dictionary's* definition for original is: "1. existing from the first, earliest. 2. being a thing from which a copy or translation has been made. 3. firsthand, not imitative; new in character or design. 4. thinking or acting for oneself, inventive, creative—an original mind." This implies that to be original you have to be the first to do something. But how can you be the first if there is nothing new under the sun?

If you take an idea, new or old, put your heart into it, and present it to the world in your own unique way, then you have created originality. When you ask a room full of children to paint a tree, a house, and a sun, you get many different representations of the same ideas. Think of being original as being purely you—creating purity—finding your creative voice. If the origin of your ideas is your heart and soul, you will be original.

Recharging Your Source

1. When you find yourself at a loss for ideas, or in a state of confusion, thinking you don't have any original ideas, it helps to take a few days off from outside input. This means: Stop

reading for a few days. Turn off the television, limit phone calls, and do everything you can to cleanse yourself of outside influence. During this time, don't bother yourself with questions. Don't ponder on the "whys." Just give yourself a break. It may be difficult, but you can do it. In place of the activities you've stopped, you can listen to music without lyrics, take walks, exercise, take naps, daydream, play with clay, paint pictures from your imagination, cook, and do anything else you can think of that doesn't use words. Ask the angels for heavenly input. At the end of your designated break from word input, you will feel renewed. If you don't feel any different, don't fret, because on some level you have recharged your creative battery.

2. If you try the above practice and like it, maybe once a week you can take a day off from reading. Once a week, turn off the TV and radio. Even if you only take an hour off, just changing your routine can help. Think of other practices that will help *you* be purely *you* and integrate them into your life as an ongoing practice.

3. Refrain from comparison. Stop the comparison game if you are playing it. There is no such thing as comparison. Each creation is a gift unto itself. Don't get "hung up" on style or originality, or you will miss it. It is impossible to copy expressions from the heart. If your heart is in what you create and others try to copy it, their attempts will be dry—not juicy and alive.

4. Be prolific. Being prolific means producing much fruit or many flowers. Think ahead with your own creativity, and keep moving. Don't stop at one or two paintings, one or two books, one or two compositions, one or two creative dinners; create, and then create again and again. This is a good way to hone your craft and create originality. Remember that rust forms

on machines that aren't used and water that is not allowed to flow becomes stagnant. Be prolific and your creative energy will flow and expand, and the angels will expand with you.

Creating Vision

Whatever you can do, or dream you can, begin it.
Boldness has genius, power, and magic in it.
Goethe

Are you hung up on the trees, entangled in the branches, or do you sense the forest? Do you see the big picture? When you are stuck among the trivial details of a creative project, how do you rise above entanglement? One way people can sabotage their creativity is to get hung up on all sorts of little details and worries and not proceed with their project or goal. A lot of these worries will only have the chance to take form *after* you have actually followed through with the project, and then you will welcome them not as worries but as problems to solve creatively. There are always plenty of things to worry about and plenty of excuses for not acting on something. The way around this is to hold a vision in your consciousness of your finished project or your ultimate idea with room for growth. The next thing is to trust that you are protected and to know that anything that happens in the future will take care of itself with the help of your own ingenuity and the angels, when the time comes. You have probably heard the saying that a journey of a thousand miles begins with a single step (forward). A creative project also has many steps, and the steps lead to your vision. Ask your angels to help you hold a vision of the big picture.

Exploring the Big Picture

1. The big picture is more than a "picture" or a vision; it is an essence. Keep an awareness that the big picture is in process and subject to "changels" (the angels of change). Hold a flexible and positive view of your personal big picture. Start to think about your overall concept and write down some thoughts.

2. Rent the movie *Creator.* The character Peter O'Toole plays talks constantly about the big picture in this delightful movie.

3. Write down a list of interferences and entanglements that keep you stuck. Next to each one, note whether or not it has happened yet or is a future possibility. If you have a present entanglement, think about how the angels can help you out of it with their vision from above. When you begin to see more of the big picture, I assure you that you won't take the little details so seriously, and you will be free to create your vision.

4. The angels are the big picture, behind-the-scenes team. Think of your part as a director or an actor, and imagine the angels playing most of the other parts. Let your imagination run with this, and keep in mind that life is one big picture.

Creating Possibilities

I believe that angels are forms, images, and expressions through which the essences and energy forces of God can be transmitted and that, since there are an infinite number of these forms, the greatest service anyone can pay the angelic host is never consciously to limit the ways angels might appear to us.

Don Gilmore, *Angels, Angels, Everywhere*

There are always possibilities. What is a possibility? Something that may exist or happen, something to be discovered. There are always positive possibilities—endless ideas of what can be discovered. Remember if you have thought of something (a possibility), it exists. One way to create possibilities is to ignore statistics. Too often, we hear gloomy statistics. Perhaps you want to sell your house, and someone informs you that you might as well forget it, because houses aren't selling on this street. Or maybe you really want to work in a career field that is overcrowded, and you hear how crazy you are for studying this field because you will never get a job and so forth. Forget the nay sayers. If you want to do something, do it, study it, create it. The possibilities for a positive outcome are there waiting for you. As the archangel Gabriel said, "For nothing will be impossible with God." (Luke 1:37).

Nothing Is Impossible!

1. If you need a solution or a plan or a goal, start brainstorming for ideas and possibilities. This will help you believe that you can rely on yourself for creative solutions. Ask the angels to help, and the possibilities will astound you.

2. If you own a business or work with others, brainstorming and listing possibilities can be very exciting when everyone gets involved and calls on the angels to help inspire them.

Creating Education

Life is a school.
Why not try taking the curriculum?
Proverb

You are now a student at the Divine University of Life, so it is time to prepare to receive higher knowledge. Be assured, spiritual knowledge is coming your way, because the angels are in school with you. They are your guidance counselors, assisting you in choosing which classes to take. The angels also help by bringing you information at the right time. Angels help you create a spiritual environment in your mind for creative thinking. The angels bring light into our minds so that we can attain clarity and do so in a joyful, positive way.

While attending the Divine University of Life, it is important that we think for ourselves and foster free thinking, especially in the spiritual arena. Thomas Jefferson once said, "I have sworn upon the altar of God, eternal hostility against every form of tyranny over the mind of man." Jefferson's political creed rested on his ultimate faith that "man" had a "capacity for improvement, for learning and understanding himself and the world." Jefferson had too much experience with human nature to trust it completely, but he was confident that under proper conditions, humans could be relied upon to think and do the right thing–if they were free, educated, and "habituated to think for themselves and to follow reason as their guides." I think the angels sometimes feel the same way about humans.

Homework

1. Think about the Divine University of Life, which the angels run, and ponder these questions: What is your major? Is it your intention to attain a master's degree or become a doctor of philosophy? Or are you just starting out with the enthusiasm and wonder of a freshman? Are you overconfident like

a sophomore? Settled in like a junior? Or just beginning to get the big picture in your senior year? Of course, this is just good old angel fun—not to be taken seriously.

2. Consider these student guidelines:

- Study what interests you.
- Stretch and exercise your mind in a comfortable way.
- Seek wisdom.
- Make friends with the library.
- Come to your own conclusions.
- Don't cheat or look for easy ways around tough assignments.
- Embrace challenge.
- Remind yourself that you are a person with a brain housing a mind that has unlimited access to energy, and rarely if ever is a brain or mind used to full capacity.

3. Create an angel study plan, a "class schedule" for your school year. There are many classes offered. Some examples include: Creative Angel Writing 201, Angelic Forgiveness Practices 101, Angel Psychology 202, and courses on other topics, such as enthusiasm, inspiration, nonattachment, communication, compassion, and so on.

4. Visualize the angels stretching your mind and energizing your brain cells, establishing direct connections to the realm of heaven.

Creating Relationships

To create means to relate. The root meaning of the word art *is to fit together and we all do this every day.*

Each time we fit things together we are creating—whether it is to make a loaf of bread, a child, a day.
Corita Kent, *Learning by Heart*

Very few things impress me more than healthy, functional human relationships. Unfortunately, the reason that I am so impressed is that true healthy relationships between people are so rare—at least by my standard and definition of *functional.*

I think we learn the most difficult lessons through our relationships with others. One reason is that we are always attracting, and attracted to, mirrors that reflect an aspect of ourselves we need to look at honestly. We have such a hard time expressing our feelings and our thoughts. One reason is that words are so limiting, and we forget to use our creativity to find new ways to express ourselves and handle our relationships.

Expressive Connections

1. Think about how you can express yourself in your relationships in new and creative ways. Discover angelic avenues that flow through your relationships, and encourage them.
2. Write, in a stream-of-consciousness fashion, about any issues you may have with particular people. Just go with the flow, and let your thoughts run deep and wide as you write.
3. Draw two pictures of someone you are close to and occasionally have difficulty understanding. These pictures are now mirrors. Inside one mirror, write aspects of that person that you are attracted to, and inside the other, write aspects that repel you or upset you. Now, pretend you are looking into these mirrors and seeing your own reflection. Don't take it too seriously

if you see something in the "negative" mirror that you need to own. Have a good laugh about it. We really are the funniest when we get into a snag with our relationships. I am forever forgiving myself for being so ridiculous and serious about not handling a relationship in the most positive way. So have some fun creating your relationships. They will bring you the most joy and fulfillment in life—and probably the most frustration. So take it lightly; it will all come out in the wash!

Creating Time Expansion

To see a world in a grain of sand,
And heaven in a wildflower,
Hold infinity in the palm of your hand,
And eternity in an hour.
William Blake

One effective way to experience the angelic realm of heaven is to play with ideas of time and space. This may be hard for those who grew up in a world of clocks and dates. Some aboriginal cultures have no clocks. They measure time as either "the now" or "all other time." You may have found yourself in a situation when time seemed suspended. Often, mystical experiences seem to stop time. In our dreams, we don't measure time. Dreams that seem to last hours may have taken only two minutes by the clock. Don't overwhelm yourself. Just begin to open your mind to the idea that "time is not linear." This is an example of a situation where words just don't do it. Plant the seed that your desire is to explore beyond the world's standards of time, and you will slowly but surely have new insights into the space and time of the angels. The angels operate outside of our time limits. They can contract and expand time when they need to.

Time Is Not Linear

1. Ask yourself some questions about your relationship to time:

- When am I acutely aware of time passing?
- When do I forget about time?
- When did I first become aware of the relativity of time?
- What other timeless moments have I experienced?
- What does "sequential flow in the moment" mean to me?

2. Experience this time meditation: Go into a meditative state with your angels, absorb the moment, and explore the realm where time doesn't exist—the realm of heaven. Explore the ideas of different vibrational levels existing in the same space. Think about the idea that everything is happening at once, right now. And remember to have fun, and keep it light and angelic. Discovering new feelings and knowledge about time concerns the freedom of your spirit. Write about your time meditation.

Creating Eclectic Likes

The artist is not a special kind of man,
but every man is a special kind of artist.
Meister Eckhart

Eclectic means choosing or accepting from various sources. A *like* is something you find pleasant and satisfactory. I think it is fun to like many different things, which don't necessarily have to follow one particular trend or trait. *Eclectic* is a word often used to describe someone's taste in music. This is because we have so many types and categories of music to choose from. Wouldn't it be awful if you had to eat the same flavor of ice cream over and over, not because you wanted to, but because you felt that eating other flavors might make people think you were a certain type of person? Well, I think it is awful when people feel that they have to listen to one type of music only. They are missing a whole world of sound delights when this happens. Music is one of the most friendly companions to our moods and emotions. Sometimes I'm in the mood to hear "oldies," but other times I get too emotional listening to songs from the past. Quite often, I listen to country music while driving and classical music or new wave music while writing.

The problem of getting stuck in a category can carry over into many areas of our lives. One big area is the type of books we read. My friends get a good laugh sometimes when they see the range of books and magazines I read. Sometimes there is no substitute for a juicy novel.

Maybe you feel that you have to dress a certain way all the time or buy all of your clothes from a certain store or catalog. Maybe because of your age or career, you think a certain hairstyle fits, when you would really just like to grow your hair as long as it can get and look wild.

Let me say here that if you are happy fitting into a category, then please don't think that I am not respecting this. I just know from experience that we can better free our playful nature by integrating a sense of the eclectic into our everyday life. I also want to reaffirm that it is okay to *like* things. I like a lot of things that others just turn their noses up at. Sometimes it takes more courage to state your likes than to state your dislikes!

I Like It!

1. Start to think of your likes and dislikes—the ones that show up over and over. Then ask the angels to help guide you to other things you may like that you may not have been open to before. Maybe this will be a person you felt you didn't have anything in common with. Maybe it will be a new food, a new book, or a new type of music. Personally I think it would be impossible to be too eclectic or to have too many likes. If people find fault with your budding eclecticism, don't take it seriously. It is better to have liked and lost than to never have liked at all! Have some fun. There are so many things in this universe to like.

2. Consider sharing your likes with a friend. Perhaps as you're taking a walk together, you can make a game out of pointing out all the things you like about what you see. This is a pleasant antidote for all the times we've done just the opposite!

Creating Religion

The most difficult thing about trusting God
is knowing God. Unfortunately, though many of us
have been taught about God, we have not been
encouraged to know God on our own terms.
Adriana Diaz, *Freeing the Creative Spirit*

Years ago, about twenty to be exact, on Christmas day two members of a religious group came to our door to inform us that

Christmas was a pagan holiday and that we were sinning by giving gifts to each other. I had just returned from a wonderful hike in the mountains, and when the doorbell rang my mother asked me to answer it. I was in a great mood and immediately wished the visitors an enthusiastic "Merry Christmas" as I opened the door. One of the two men broke into a smile, but the other one was very serious and wanted me to know about the dangers of celebrating a pagan holiday. He then wanted me to know about his religion, but I told him that I had recently formed my own religion and that it included giving gifts and celebrating ourselves because we are so wonderful. This was a spontaneous statement, because I hadn't really formed my own religion–at least I didn't realize it at the time. I have always believed that we are all wonderful and should give gifts to celebrate the fact, so in essence I have always followed the belief system of the religion I started that day.

The visitors left, seeming a bit confused. The man who had smiled had actually laughed a couple of times as I told them how satisfied I was with my religion. I came back with statements to assure them that I didn't need their religion and that I was okay and not too worried about the sixty-day notice they were giving me for the end of the world. I had a lot of fun that day playing with the idea that I had my own special religion. Because it was so fun, I've secretly played with the idea for the last twenty years.

If you look up the word *religion* in the dictionary, you'll find it simply means a belief in the existence of a superhuman controlling power, especially of God, usually expressed in worship, and is used to define a particular system of faith and worship, such as the Christian religion. It seems so odd to me that such a simple concept has caused such serious problems throughout history.

Creating your own religion is a good way to free your spirit and "know God on your own terms." Of course, this doesn't mean that you can't belong to an organized religion and have your own, too. Creating your own religion can be something you do in private, and this way you can change and adjust your religious beliefs as you grow and expand. This is not something to take seriously—just something to have fun with and get you thinking in a freer way about who you are and what you believe.

Freedom of Religion

1. One of the guiding impulses of the archangel Michael is free thinking. Michael sends us inspiration that urges us to open our minds to new ways of thinking and encourages us to figure out for ourselves where we need to be and how to get there. Creating our own religion can help us free our thinking and figure things out for ourselves. Think about ways the angels can help you form your own religion in a fun and humorous way. Look at the books you read, think about your beliefs, and start to pull together the information in a way you feel defines your religion.

2. In the quotation at the beginning of this section, Adriana Diaz brings up an important point: "The most difficult thing about trusting God is knowing God." Think of ways you could create your own religion to be one of truly knowing God. Think of times you feel especially close to God and bring new awareness to these times. For example, if you feel close to God in your garden, go to your garden and ask yourself if you know

God. Ask the angels to help you know God in your everyday life, so that you can fully trust God.

Creating Talent

There is no such thing as talent, only awareness.
Chogyam Trungpa

Could we really create talent? Isn't talent something we are born with, something that we have no choice over? Well, to tell you the truth, I'm not sure. But in this world of endless possibilities, I think we can create talent if we expand our view of what talent is and if we bring the angels in on our quest. The official definition of *talent* is "special or very great ability." *Ability* is "the quality that makes an action or process possible, or the cleverness and the capacity to do something."

I truly believe that we are born with an abundance of ability and capability. I would use the word *potential* here, but I'm waging a personal boycott of that word because I think it points to something that is not present. We use the word *potential* to excuse or criticize people at times. So what if people have potential? All that really matters is what they are doing now. Humans really are amazing and seldom fully aware of the capabilities they do have. Some people come back from near-death experiences with new talents or abilities to do something that they didn't have before. Sometimes the angels come to people and ask them to create something they never thought they could have created. So expand your ideas about talent, and ask the angels for rebirth if you think that we are born with only a set amount.

Angels as Talent Agents

1. Think about your own talents and abilities and list them. Ask yourself whether you were born with these talents or acquired them through the course of your life. Then list how the angels could help you expand your present talents and bring more talents to you in other areas. I have heard it said that we express our guardian angel's talent. So our guardian angel wants us to be the very best and have the very best chances. Think of your guardian angel as your talent agent, and have fun!

2. Review the list of your talents and abilities. Think of ways the angels could give you courage to expand and trust more in your talents.

Creating Spiritual Sleep

We are so captivated by and entangled in our subjective consciousness that we have forgotten the age-old fact that God speaks chiefly through dreams and visions.
C. G. Jung

Our spiritual life doesn't stop when we go to sleep; it flourishes and nourishes itself. Dreamtime is spirit time and offers a great opportunity to play with the angels. Many artists find that they are given direct inspiration for their art through their dreams. I knew a musician, when we were both in high school, who had dreams of sheet music written out. He would wake up and write down the notes and then incorporate them into a song the next day. Dreams give us insight into our life journey, guiding and pointing us in the direction of our true inner self and toward whatever we need to look at, resolve, create, or transmute.

Dreams are a good way to realize that we are not in control and that this is okay! When you fall asleep, you enter a world where you are at the mercy of your unconscious mind. If you have had trouble with the issue of surrender in your waking life, remember that each time you sleep you have truly surrendered.

Spiritual Sleep Ideas

1. Have a favorite scent nearby to sniff when you sleep. Make sure there is fresh air in your bedroom.

2. Visualize a door to the angelic realm, and as you fall asleep imagine it opening and allowing passage for you and the angels to play.

3. Listen to a guided meditation or soothing music as you journey into the land of sleep.

4. Avoid watching world or local news on television right before bedtime, as this tends to disturb your sleep time.

5. Right before going to sleep, softly focus on a creative project you are involved in. Perhaps write about your goals, visions, hopes, and so forth. Then ask the angels to bring you insight and inspiration for your project during dream time. In the morning, write about your project again, especially if you recall a dream concerning it.

6. Play with creative ways to sleep spiritually. The angels are near when you go to sleep. They can help you clear the day's troubles away and give you a warm tingling feeling as you float away softly into angelic dreamland.

7. As for dream interpretation, you are the best interpreter of your own dreams. Don't take too much stock in dream dictionary definitions. Allow the angels to help you interpret your dreams.

Creating Room for Spirit

Holy Spirit, giving life to all life, moving all creatures,
root of all things, washing them clean, wiping out
their mistakes, healing their wounds, you are
our true life, luminous, wonderful,
awakening the heart from its ancient sleep.
Hildegard of Bingen

The free spirit wants in. Spirit will find its way into your creativity however it can. Spirit gives life to our creativity. Spirit must move through something that is already alive, ready to receive it. The human touch is conducive to the flow of spirit. When I was studying art as a child, my teacher took a ruler away from me when I was going to make a straight line and said, "The eye is the best measuring instrument." I didn't really understand at the time, because as a child I had trouble drawing a straight line, but now I understand the essence of what my teacher meant. Another art teacher told me that there are no absolutely straight lines in nature. The underlying message was to draw and create what is inside ourselves without perfection and measurement. In *Guardians of Hope,* I discussed the issue of not striving or straining for perfection. I used an example of Amish quilters, who always make sure one patch doesn't match the rest in a finished quilt. They do this to remind themselves that the Creator does not make anyone "perfect." They believe that this mismatched patch is where spirit enters the creation. At Findhorn garden, the gardeners leave a space to grow wild so that the natural spirit of the landscape can live without human intervention.

As you play with this idea, I hope it helps free you from the confines of perfection as it has freed me. These days many of us are attracted to unusual items that are handmade, homemade, or give the essence of coming from the heart and hands. When mass-market advertisers try to copy this essence with their slick ads, it just doesn't work. The reason is that spirit must enter a creation to make it alive, to allow it to share the spirit of life with all. To transmit the joy and love of the creative spirit, something has to touch our hearts and souls, not just our minds.

True perfection exists only in everything being just what it is. Nothing more, nothing less. The universe is perfect, but we always want to impose limits and project our own ideas onto it. To allow spirit to enter our creations, we need to express what is in us, without judgment, for the pure love of creation. In this way spirit will fill our lives and our souls.

Sing to Yourself: "I've Got the Spirit!"

1. Think of people you know who have a lot of spirit and share it wherever they go. Do they follow all the rules and regulations of behaving properly? Do they follow societal mores? When people are truly enthusiastic and alive, are they stopping to worry about everyone else's reactions? Perfect behavior is another joke—another issue of control. We want to be in control, so we try to make people behave in a certain manner, when

spirit actually wants them to be free and wild and to learn their own lessons. Think about any rules you have regarding behavior, and let go of them. If you feel you are restricted by rules you don't like, make up your own set of rules—for yourself only, please. Ask the angels for constant reassurance that it is okay to be spirited, and they will be there to help you express with spirit.

2. Think about your physical appearance and any imperfections you feel you have, if that applies. Now think of these so called imperfections as places where your spirit communicates and flows. We are not loved because of the way we look; there is no such thing as conditional love—it is impossible. Be loving, and you will have love; give love, and you will get love; be yourself, and you will be loved as such; try to be something else, and you will always be out of reach of the purity of true love.

3. When you create something, make sure there is a "spirit point" (like the mismatched patch on the Amish quilts). This spirit point can take any form you like: You could send something off with a coffee stain, a misspelled word, or a typo, or you could put a blob of color on a painting where it doesn't seem to fit. Don't take this process too seriously or try too hard; just keep in mind that you want spirit to enter your creation, and it needs a point of entry. The angels will help you get over the "it has to be perfect" syndrome. P.S. We usually add a spirit point without even realizing it!

4. Simplicity leads to longevity. Sometimes we associate simple things with a lack of substance or intelligence, but I have found the opposite to be true. Wisdom finds an inviting resting place in simplicity. Keeping things simple allows much room for spirit. Complexity can be draining and stressful, so it is wise

to cultivate simplicity at times. Think of how you can simplify your creativity. Don't make this into a rigid rule, because complex creativity also has its place; just give yourself the option to keep things simple when appropriate.

Creating an Angel Journal

The point of practicing an art is less to discover who you are than to become your truth, to be able to shed all sham, imposture and bluff in relation to yourself and others. True art is not an indulgence of the little self, but a manifestation of the Self.
Frederick Franck, *Art as a Way*

Keeping a journal allows you to create a safe place to express your true self, to express your truth. By writing in a journal, you get to know yourself with the goal of loving yourself and life in a full, rewarding way. In your journal, you can experiment with any form of written or artistic expression you would like. There are no rules or regulations for what you choose to do with your journal. The goals you set are yours and yours alone. A journal encourages you not only to know yourself but to know the unseen world of the angels, who are there to inspire and guide you every day of your life. When I became conscious of the angels in my life, I immediately began a new journal to keep track of my spiritual growth and the ways in which the angels were helping me. That particular journal became the idea source for the book *Messengers of Light.*

In *Messengers of Light,* I suggested keeping an angel journal for several reasons. Mainly, I feel that keeping a journal is a great way to get to know the angels in your life in your own way. Each of us is unique, and the angels play unique roles in our lives. When I started to expand my own angel consciousness, I couldn't find many books or people offering the knowledge I was looking for about angels. So I took basic spiritual ideas and principles and played with the idea that angels are our spiritual helpers, interested in guiding us to our highest spiritual good. I also discovered the many other wonderful things angels do. As my angel consciousness expands, I keep writing.

Learn to discern what is right *for you* through journal keeping. This may change, grow, and expand over time. Allow the growth. Keeping an angel journal will help advance your quest for your own inner truth about the angels. Sometimes my original thoughts or beliefs about angels change as I gather more information. But the basic feelings I have about the angels haven't changed. These feelings include:

- The angels represent the highest divine love in the universe.
- They are a direct link for us to God, the ultimate Creator.
- They are separate beings of light, love, and joy.
- When angels come into our lives and consciousness we experience lessons of love that encourage us to grow beyond our wildest dreams.
- Angels help us to express our own spiritual creativity by inspiring us through the energy system of love.

Whenever you find yourself blocked or stuck, ask the angels to help remind you that you are a free, creative soul, with infinite access to rich treasures of amazing ideas you can reach through your own imagination.

Ideas to Develop in Your Angel Journal

1. Take your journal out in the world with you. Take a nap with your journal. Meditate with your journal. Be best friends with your journal. Allow your journal to be an extension of you or your energy, a bit like a pet. And, most of all, have fun with your journal.

2. Here are some helpful journal companions and tools to have on hand:

- A compass for drawing circles
- Colored pencils
- A special pen with colored ink you resonate with
- Calligraphy pens and ink, if this interests you
- A glue stick
- Music
- Scents to inspire
- Candles
- Stones and other objects meaningful to you
- Highlighting marker to highlight impact revelations
- A journal box for storing tools, pictures for collages, and other accessories

3. You may find that after a while your journal is looking more like a scrapbook. That's great; go with it! Or you may keep a companion scrapbook or sketchbook to go with your journal. Think about items you'd like to keep, such as pressed flowers, ribbons, leaves from a special walk, angel stickers, and so forth. If you are so inspired, glue these in your journal and write a story about them. Color-copying photos and slides is a good way to present them in your journal.

4. Thoughts are free; angels are God's thoughts, and so are we. In your journal, explore the idea of thoughts becoming form.

5. Find favorite pictures of angels, photos where strange lights have appeared, and inspiring drawings, and paste them in your journal wherever and whenever you please.

6. Write about yourself and your guardian angel in the third person.

7. List favorite angel books with comments as your own reference guide.

8. Include quotations about angels that inspire you. Or pick a topic, such as happiness, and find quotations about it.

9. Has the light increased in the world around you? How does this light affect you and influence your life situations? Keep a page to note your observations of light and the changes happening around you.

10. Pick messages from your heart, affirmations, and ideas about yourself that you like. Choose one each week to be your special affirmation and paste it where you'll see it every day.

Chapter 2
Spiritual Integrity

I want to go on living even after my death! And therefore I am grateful to God for giving me this gift, this possibility of developing myself, and of writing, of expressing all that is within me.
Anne Frank

Spiritual integrity is creative wholeness. We are creators, and we have the choice to create a beautiful spiritual existence for ourselves. At some point, we experience a revelation and the angels show us that to be truly happy is to be of service to the Creator out of joy and love. Our lives then become a creative journey for the glory of God.

Spiritual creativity is a way of life, a way of wholeness. It is a path of integrity. Integrity entails not just a few beliefs or specific acts, but an attitude that we adopt and practice in our everyday lives. Loving yourself—falling back in love with yourself as a child of God—is the first step in the process of spiritual integrity. The word *process* is important; this is not an overnight or a sudden change you make in your life, but rather an ongoing process that can bring you much joy.

I know in my heart that the angels want us to cocreate more hope, joy, beauty, peace, and love for the world. If we took all of these wonderful qualities out of the picture, we would have a gray, dreary world with few happy people. Sometimes when

I watch the news or pay too close attention to the negative events in the world, I start to think the beautiful aspects of life are becoming extinct. It is up to us to keep hope, joy, beauty, peace, and love alive on the earth, and the best way we can do this is with our own creativity. For example, think about how wonderful it is when you see that others have taken the time to plant some flowers either in their own yards or in public spaces. Think of how you feel when you read a book, watch a movie, or view a painting that gives you hope and touches your heart. Think about how different you make the world when you leave your home having created a peaceful aura about you.

Is there any better feeling than truly expressing your own special brand of love to the world? This takes spiritual integrity—walking your talk—and the angels teach you this integrity through creativity. Let the angels know that you are willing to help them increase the light and cocreate beauty, love, hope, joy, and peace on earth. The angels are actively recruiting volunteers now, and they have chosen you.

Creating a Masterpiece

Every person is special; everyone who exists
is a unique thought of God.
K. Martin-Kuri

Creating your life as a work of art—a masterpiece—is a lifelong process. Life is not like instant soup—pour in boiling water and there you have it. Creating your life and yourself as a work of great art requires commitment and intention over time. Often in our society, we tend to look for quick fixes: Put a little sugar on top, paint over the flaws, win friends and manipulate people, build a house overnight with inferior materials—all of it so that we can slide by to the next day and possibly end up with some money or power to show for it. The quick-fix trend is now so blatant that commercials come right out and portray empty people trying to manipulate and gain control without anything real to back them up. We have lost the essence of greatness in our society. We have become unreal, unable to express our true selves because we aren't even sure what that means. Too often we seek shortcuts to some utopia we've fantasized about in our minds. We end up blocking ourselves from seeing what is right in front of us, demanding our true attention.

Stephen R. Covey, in his best-selling book *The Seven Habits of Highly Effective People,* reveals the following:

> I began to feel more and more that much of the success literature of the past 50 years was superficial. It was filled with social image consciousness, techniques and quick fixes—with social band-aids and aspirin that addressed acute problems and sometimes even appeared to solve them temporarily, but left the underlying chronic problems untouched to fester and resurface time and again. In stark contrast, almost all the literature in the first 150 years or so focused on what could be called the Character Ethic as the foundation of success—things like integrity, humility, fidelity, temperance, courage, justice, patience, industry, simplicity, modesty, and the Golden Rule.

It is time to start rebuilding our basic characters. I have to admit that when I first started having fun with the angels,

I tended to view them as shortcuts around pain and problems—as a force I could depend on to "make it all better." Well, I was partly right. The angels are a force to depend on, but they *don't* make it all better; rather, they help guide us to use our own ingenuity and resolve our own problems as we cocreate with them. There aren't any shortcuts around pain. There are no quick fixes. Eventually the piper must be paid, but the angels can help us get beyond just wanting the pain gone. They can help us change our perceptions of problems and pain, so that even our internal chemistry shifts to a much lighter state. Many people who have studied angelology or who have lived in angel consciousness for a long time say that the angels are interested in helping us become great people with integrity and strength, so that we can be a guiding light for others. The angels want to help us create our personal lives as masterpieces as we cocreate heavenly qualities with the Creator.

A masterpiece is something that exudes true mastery. You have probably heard stories of people going through college to train for a particular career, and then, when they get out into the real world, they find that they haven't been taught some of the basic principles that their job demands. Well, many of us haven't been taught some of the basic principles that life demands. We haven't been taught to develop character and strength. One reason is that there are very few great role models. One way to learn greatness and integrity is to be taught by the examples of those who have embodied these qualities. Who is really teaching this? Sometimes it seems that many of our leaders and teachers are more concerned with getting their names out than they are with the message of mastery and greatness that we as humans are here to achieve. We can teach ourselves. The answers are etched on our souls, and the angels can help us access the character building blocks that we need in our lives. In fact, they present many lessons for us, and the answers to the questions we confront offer clues to what our basic characters need in order to be great and strong. Greatness has little or nothing to do with fame. Some of the greatest people I have met may never achieve fame, but they will certainly leave a positive, light-filled mark on the planet. If you meet up with someone who is obsessed with gaining recognition or fame, I recommend turning the corner fast; you will not receive true wisdom from such a source.

Creating character is also a process of becoming more angelic. By angelic, I don't mean becoming or continuing to be "nice." "Niceness" is a screen we use to control and to decide whether we like others. "Oh, they are so nice," we say. What does this mean? Usually it means that they have done just what we wanted them to do. Angels aren't always "nice," meaning they don't always do exactly what we want them to do. No matter what, the angels are always true to the Creator. Angels cannot ignore the basic principles that build strength of character. Even if there were an easy way out, they wouldn't provide it. Angels are always loving, and they want us to start finding pure love, which is a basic energy, not a condition of "niceness" and being liked by others. Becoming angelic doesn't mean pleasing everyone; it means staying true to yourself, your values, your integrity, your Creator. If you think you don't have values, integrity, or a Creator, then this may seem impossible to you, but even so you can begin to develop integrity and become aware of your values and your Creator. The angels are here to help you.

One of God's Very Best

1. At a fair once, I saw a very creative sign that said something like, "One of God's Very Best Masseurs." I thought this was a brilliant slogan, and he was definitely one of God's very best! Think of yourself as one of God's very best in your own life. The angels love to play this game with you, and they can actively guide you to be one of God's very best. So, complete the following sentence: I am one of God's very best ______.

2. Think about how your life and your creative service are part of the Creator. Think about ways to be more of a piece of the Creator, and integrate these practices into your everyday life.

Creating Self-Love

What lies behind us and what lies before us are tiny matters compared to what lies within us.
Henry David Thoreau

Thoreau's saying rings so true. What lies within us? Ask yourself what lies within you. Make a list if you want. I know that within all of us is the light of God. Suppose I came along and handed you a clear glass vase and told you it was filled with an actual part of God. Inside this vase you'd see the most beautiful and unique color of light brought forth straight from the realm of heaven. As this special light was put into the vase, the angels blessed it and carefully brought it to earth. Now you'd have the vase in your keeping. What would you do? This vase would be priceless—so valuable you would never let it out of your sight or awareness. You would cherish this vase of God and probably let only certain people near it. You would protect it from harm and make sure it didn't break. It would be the most important item to you because it represented an actual part of the light of God and you owned it.

Well, that is exactly what you are—a vessel of actual God light. How do we usually treat our part of God? Sometimes we forget we are made of God, and we are less careful with ourselves than we would be with our valuables. *You* are precious and priceless. God needs your light to shine brightly with love for your self—for God.

Understanding fully who we are and what we are doing here involves being able and willing to love ourselves. This doesn't mean loving ourselves as soon as we do a few things to make ourselves lovable; it means loving ourselves right now. We may ignore or deny this love, but the truth is we can love ourselves at this very moment in time. This may seem so simple, yet we all know how difficult it can be. The angels are very active in the lives of humans right now. Many people are seeking the spiritual dimension, and whether or not they realize it, they are attracting angels. The main lesson the angels have for us is that we are love, we are God on earth, and it is time to love ourselves and open our hearts.

I have heard many people share experiences of feeling different from their peers, family, and society from a very young age. Usually they have a story about how at one time or another they decided to explore their individuality, with seemingly disastrous results. One story in particular comes to mind. Olivia was in first grade, and the first graders were supposed to be angels for a Christmas play. The teacher gave instructions that all the angels were to be dressed in white. Olivia didn't pay attention closely to these instructions; her mind was most likely in a more creative space. So, she told her mother to make her a blue angel costume. Well, I'm sure you can finish the story; suffice it to say that her blue costume did not go over well with her teacher, and Olivia ended up feeling humiliated. I also know that you could finish the story in a much more positive way, where Olivia was accepted and maybe even rewarded for her creative statement.

Those of us like Olivia need to reward ourselves for our individualism and creativity and begin to expand it. Most highly artistic people (sometimes called "sensitives") have had difficulties adjusting to life as human beings. Sometimes it seems as if life is a series of bombardments we need to duck and hide from. Noise, negative people, pollution, rigid beliefs, and a host of other "antisensitive" occurrences make it difficult for ultra-sensitive humans to stay awake and aware. One of the main reasons the angels are closer to the earth right now is to assist sensitive people in loving themselves and understanding their sensitivity. We, as sensitives (and I know that anyone reading this book is a sensitive to some extent), have to remain strong, centered, and at peace—we must heal ourselves with self-love and learn how to balance our sensitive natures—if we are to assist in healing others.

Come to think of it, if all human beings on earth today truly loved and cared about themselves, you wouldn't recognize the planet. At the core of each unkind, selfish, greedy, or generally negative act that people commit is a lack of self-love and self-respect. Negative acts are done to fill a void within, one that was created long ago when the perpetrators were taught they had to accomplish something sensational before they could possibly receive love or self-respect. Instead of receiving unconditional love, they were led to believe that everything in the world is conditional–based mostly on how people meet conditions, as opposed to how wonderful they are inside.

Why is it that we don't all just naturally love and take good care of ourselves? Is it because we eventually die? Or because we are treated badly at times? Or because we feel no one truly loves or respects us and therefore we feel unlovable? Perhaps we were told not to promote ourselves–to be humble. Maybe we don't feel good physically and are sick much of the time, so we find it hard to love ourselves because of our physical condition. Maybe we tell ourselves we aren't "successful." Or we're ashamed of ourselves. Maybe we point to our "bad track record"–the ways we have hurt others and now blame ourselves. From a compassionate viewpoint, these reasons not to love ourselves don't make sense, but they have led many of us to think or believe that we are not worthy of self-love.

Some people blame their lack of self-love on a concrete circumstance in their lives–such as a parent they clashed with, or a negative family and education system. But blaming others or blaming circumstances doesn't ultimately heal us or lead to self-love in the present. It is okay to go back in the past, with a loving heart, with the intention of gaining an understanding of where the lack began. Sometimes we can't do this on our own, and many good counselors and therapists are available to guide us on journeys into our pasts for more understanding of ourselves. But blame ranks right up there with guilt as a growth blocker. So if you choose to go into your past, remember that your perception of the past is due mostly to your present frame of mind. If you are happy and at peace within, you may find you view your childhood and past as happy and peaceful—remembering mostly "good" things. If you are in turmoil, you will see through a lens of unhappiness and misery. So be aware!

Actually, you are very lucky if you have had a hard time loving yourself due to your past. I will tell you why. As is the case with any tough lesson, when we get through it, we are stronger and more knowledgeable. Knowledge brings awareness, and awareness means choice. Many of us create a whole framework of armor to protect us from our pain. This armor consists of denial, lies, and concepts concerning who we think we are in the world. But once you choose to love yourself, you will never be the same. Self-love brings forth the reflection of your angelic nature. Self-love connects you to the realm of heaven and brings the angels closer to your heart. By giving full attention to loving yourself, you are reborn as your true self. The angels will be so closely integrated into your life that everything you do will become an angel experience.

A spiritual path is actually a path of self-awareness. The potential for pain from lessons is based mostly on our degree of willingness to look at ourselves honestly. If we deny or ignore messages that impel us to look honestly at ourselves and our lives, unresolved issues grow larger and are harder to deal with. One could use the analogy of a tumor: The more we ignore it, and its underlying causes, the bigger it gets and the more problems it causes us.

So right now, let's cut the tumor out so that it no longer exists anywhere. We have no more reasons not to love ourselves. Begin to practice loving yourself now, regardless of what is going on in your life and regardless of all the negative thoughts that may arise. Forget them! Leave them all behind. They will drop off naturally as you begin to allow self-love to expand in your life. Believe it: The key to solving problems or issues you don't want in your life is to increase self-love and establish it as a constant practice. If you wait until all your issues are resolved to love yourself, you will wait too long. The only way the issues get resolved or dissolved is through self-love.

What exactly is self-love? What is the self? The first question should actually be: What is love? Love is God—the highest power in the universe. You are made of God—of love. The light of God is within you. Love is a big part of what you are, even if you don't consciously practice love. Remember, you are a precious treasure of love, and the angels are here to help you protect yourself—your love. Take good care of your special self; you are worth it.

The Power of Self-Love

1. Love yourself right now, not tomorrow, not when you think you are ready. Love yourself now! Self-love is totally possible and within your power. With everything you do—as you breathe, eat, drink, walk, run, clean house, and play—do it with the power of self-love. Incorporate self-love into all realms of your life.

2. Ask your guardian angel to remind you of your willingness to love yourself whenever you begin to go in the opposite direction. Your angel will gently urge you to remember to love yourself by sending you messages, so tune in.

3. Take a walk in the park with your guardian angel and think of nothing except how you love yourself. Do a walking

self-love meditation. Talk to yourself about how you are loved. Imagine your guardian angel walking right beside you, listening and agreeing with everything you say.

4. Be kind to yourself.

5. Design your own series of self-love affirmations. Pick one affirmation each week, and paste it around in places where you'll see it every day. Take it with you during the day, and say it to yourself at night right before you fall asleep. Hear your guardian angel repeat it back to you.

Creating a Meaningful Relationship With Your Own Guardian Angel

The difference from a person and an angel is easy:
Most of an angel is in the inside
and most of a person is on the outside.
Anna, in *Mister God, This Is Anna*

To create a great relationship with your own guardian angel and any other angel for that matter, you need to create a fertile and rich inner life. Creating an inner life is easy for some and more difficult for others. Some of us may spend too much time dwelling on inner-life issues, while others of us run around never stopping to hear our inner voices. All of us have an inner life; it is a matter of paying attention to it and giving it strength. Communicating with your angelic entourage is easier when you take the time to feed your inner spirit. We all have angels around us, and we have had a guardian angel with us since we first came into existence. Enjoying the full benefits of our relationships with our guardian angels means different things to different people.

So find your own creative ways to communicate, and the angels will become your intimate friends and cheerleaders.

Relating to Your Angels

1. Finish the following sentences in your journal, and begin to define your angelic connection in your own personal way.

- To me angels are . . .
- I know I have a guardian angel because . . .
- My guardian angel's purpose in my life is to . . .
- My guardian angel has a (circle one and discuss if needed) feminine/masculine/androgynous nature/essence/vibration.
- These colors come to my mind when I have a strong connection with my guardian angel (list or draw the colors):
- My favorite scent, which reminds me of my guardian angel, is . . .
- To improve my personal relationship with my guardian angel, I could engage in the following practices (for example, bringing flowers in the house, being kind, laughing):
- My guardian angel's name is (you don't really need to know a name, but some people truly enjoy having a name to call their guardian angel) . . .
- My guardian angel helps me express myself by . . .
- I also feel other angels around me helping me and my guardian angel. My experience of other angels is . . .
- The most important gift the angels have brought to me so far is . . .
- My most profound, angelically inspired, spiritual insight(s) attained so far is/are . . .

- Life-changing angel experiences and events in my life so far include . . .
- Being "spiritually creative" means . . .

2. Let yourself practice and explore. A spiritual practice can be anything from taking a walk in the woods and painting a beautiful picture to fasting and attending spiritual gatherings on a regular basis. Remember that these practices are personal to you; you are unlike any other creature in the way in which you express love to the Creator. Spiritual practices can help you connect strongly with your guardian angel. Think of some creatively spiritual ways you can put your relationship with your guardian angel into practice.

3. A muse is an angel who inspires our creative fire and encourages us to express and to purify our expression. Begin to explore the universe of creative thought with your muse. You may find your muse has a certain "voice." If this is so, pay attention, even when the thoughts don't make sense. However, don't let your muse lead you astray. Some muses have been known to be tricksters at times.

4. One way the angels can communicate with us is through synchronisms. A synchronism is a coincidence for which you recognize that a higher order exists through a sign or symbol contained in the coincidence. Keep a list of synchronisms you experience and any message you feel was relayed to you through them.

5. It's important to keep track of special angel moments that are personal to you. They don't have to be explained or confirmed by anyone. They only need to have meaning to you. When you have recorded them in your journal, you can go back

and remind yourself that you are not alone and that grace abounds.

6. Have talks with your guardian angel in your imagination. Take a walk and pretend you are talking to an invisible friend in your mind. Ask questions and you will receive answers.

Creating Play

Enthusiasm is grounded in play, not work. Far from being a brain-numbed soldier, our artist is actually our child within, our inner playmate. As with all playmates, it is joy, not duty, that makes for a lasting bond.
Julia Cameron, *The Artist's Way*

If someone asked me what I thought the most important aspect of creativity was, I would have to say the essence of "play." Play is the most important component to my own creativity. Play is also the key to truly learning anything. If we all had been allowed to learn everything with a sense of play, we would experience so much creative freedom we would not recognize the world. Think about it. Weren't we really just told what to learn and believe in school? Let's say every day the teacher brought in art materials, books, and creative props that somehow represented something we were studying and said, "Okay, class, let's spend the day playing with these so we can learn about such-and-such." What do you think would happen? My fantasy is that all the students would become teachers through their own creativity, and the class would teach itself with the main teacher directing. I also believe that teaching by play would allow people the freedom and courage to search for their own unique answers. This type of teaching is being practiced in a few innovative classrooms today. The main point is that we learn through play. This is why some children develop basic computer skills so quickly: They see computers as toys and feel free to play with them.

You were a child once and you had a natural tendency to play at all times. That child that you were is still part of you now. And that child is trying to get the message through to the adult in you that you must play again, in everything you do. When children start to have trouble and act out, one technique therapists use to discover the root problem is called play therapy. Virginia M. Axline, a pioneer in this field, wrote two very powerful books on the subject, *Dibs: In Search of Self* and *Play Therapy*. *Dibs: In Search of Self* is one of the books I will always have with me; it is a story of a miracle, a case study of play therapy. In *Play Therapy,* a seven-year-old boy is quoted during a session as saying, "Oh, every child just once in his life should have a chance to spill out all over without a 'Don't you dare! Don't you dare! Don't you dare!'" Go for it, spill out all over, create your own play therapy, leave the critics behind, and step into the safe world you can create through play.

Whenever I start to use the word *work* in my writings, I put a slash next to it and then follow it with the word *play*. Work is really adult play, but we forget this and treat our work as something stressful and serious. I believe that all human beings are created to be creative. To express ourselves, in our own special way, means unleashing our innate creativity by playing the game of life.

Playing for Health

1. Playing is a good way to stop taking things so seriously, to stop worrying, and to find a creative way to take action on our dislikes. If something is annoying you, think of how you could play with your annoyance. You could pretend it is a kite and go outside and fly it. You could turn it into a ball and bounce it so high that it leaves the universe. Make a clay object representing your annoyance and then turn it into something else right before your eyes.

2. Remember, you are a kid at heart. To be happy, you must play, play, and then play some more. Play is the way the angels communicate with us. If you are feeling lonely and you desire a playmate, you have one always waiting on call—your guardian angel.

Creating Harmony

Only those who partake of the harmony within their souls know the harmony that runs through nature.
Paramahansa Yogananda

If you know even a little bit about music and its structure and why we enjoy it, you know about harmony. When musical notes don't harmonize, this creates a tense, harsh, or discordant sound. Such a sound can be interesting and create excitement, so I am not saying here that harmony is good and discordance necessarily bad; creativity can embrace both.

Recently as I was talking with my friend Shannon, we realized that each of us has an inner note that our soul sings. When we are in tune with the divine, our note resonates with the harmony of heaven and the choirs of angels. We can use this idea in our personal relationships. Some people we find ourselves in perfect harmony with, and others seem to be part of a different scale.

Harmonious living means forming a pleasing or consistent whole, free from disagreement or ill feeling. To create a harmonious whole with our lives and the people we encounter, we need to find the point of harmony between us and them. Of course, we can learn much from those who don't harmonize with our inner note, but the more aware we are of what is going on, the better we can create harmony in our lives, which may mean keeping a healthy distance from certain people. We will notice harmony best if we allow ourselves to open our hearts more. If we find that there is no harmony and that all we see is drama or dysfunction, we can still keep this discordance out of our inner sanctums.

When we practice a spiritual life and include prayer, contemplation, meditation, spiritual study, self-awareness, compassion, and service as a constant part of our lives, we are resonating to a spiritual scale of musical notes. When we encounter people who are not practicing spiritual lives, even if they say they are, our notes won't resonate harmonically. If we try to work in partnership with someone who is only in it for money and glamour, and we are in it for love, service, and creativity, we won't find harmony.

Have you ever noticed how colors don't clash in nature? We can mix purples, oranges, yellows, and reds along with greens, and as long as the combination is part of nature it will never clash. Well, if we are natural and spiritual, it won't matter how many different notes we get together; as long as we are in tune with the divine, we will be in harmony. All of this is another idea to play with for understanding. If it makes sense to you, see if you can play with it in your own life.

Getting a Tune-up

1. Keep your inner note strong by keeping it in tune. You can do this by staying true to yourself and not trying to fit with another note that is not in harmony with yours. Ask the angels to remind you when you need to tune up your inner note.

2. Listen to the chord struck between two souls. Think of relationships you have in your life, and go into a meditative state with the angels. Get in touch with your own inner note. It is okay if you don't hear a tone—just use your imagination. Now listen to the notes of other people in your life. Do they harmonize? After you meditate on harmony, write about your thoughts. If you find that you don't harmonize with someone, think about why. The answer is probably a matter of values clashing.

3. If you put your heart into it, your creativity and your life will resonate with other hearts and attract true appreciation.

4. Investigate harmonic resonance in your own life and in your creative expression. You may find that leading a harmonious life will get you in touch with the key that unlocks the door to your creative heart center. The angels know right where this key is at all times.

5. Create your own "harmonic convergence" in your life with the angels.

Creating Happiness

True happiness is the ability, developed over time and with practice, to radiate positive energy regardless of external or internal circumstances.
Dan Millman, *No Ordinary Moments*

Guess what—the news is out—you can actually be in a happy state even if everything in your life is not perfect. You can even be happy if you are feeling sick and in pain. And you are even allowed to have other emotions, such as anger or sadness, and still be happy. All you have to do is know and believe that you don't need any particular reason to be happy. Happiness is bigger than our body, expands beyond our mind, and is a current of life force energy that is with us at all times. Attaining happiness is the driving force behind many things humans do, but the truth is we won't achieve happiness by driving or trying, only by allowing its energy to flow with us and be part of us.

Tuning Into the Flow of Happiness

1. Happiness to me is the same as grace. We cannot do anything to attain grace—only be available to experience and receive. Start exploring happiness without reason in your own way. Keep tuning in to it when you start to feel it come over you. Each time, you will find it easier to identify, and pretty soon it will always be with you—right under the surface of all you do and go through.

2. Happiness is a state of being that is always with you, just like the angels. The angels hold a part of you in the flow of happiness at all times. When you are feeling down, remember that at anytime you can reconnect with the flow of happiness. You can even allow yourself to laugh during a sad moment.

3. Be happy, don't worry, and "whistle while you work" (play).

Creating Fun

Laughter is the audio announcement that Fun is being had. In its fullest form laughter is both healthy and holy. If you don't have a sense of humor it just isn't funny any more.
Wavy Gravy, *Something Good for a Change*

Recently I realized that I hadn't had fun for a very long time. Then I realized that many of the things I used to do that I thought were fun no longer appealed to me or no longer fit my life-style. So I started to think about fun and what it really means. Does it mean doing something specific, or is it a quality that can be brought into most any activity?

When I think about fun and play, I can't help but think of children. One thing I have noticed about happy, well-adjusted children is that they all have a very unique sense of humor and expressing their sense of humor is important to them. It is a big part of the way they interact with adults and one another. Why do you think children laugh so much when they are having fun together? Laughter is very important to adults, too. Humor is one of the main ways the angels communicate with us.

Funny

1. Use “flash thoughts” to answer the following. Flash thoughts are thoughts that come quickly to you when you begin to ponder a subject. Record the thoughts and ideas that pop into your mind as you think about the following.

- Write down your first thoughts about fun.
- List some fun activities.
- Is play different from fun? If so, how and why?
- What does *frolic* mean to you?
- Have you frolicked lately?
- Do the angels have fun?

2. Think about humor and laughter and their role in your life lately. Write a few thoughts down.

3. Keep a mental tab on how often you laugh during the day.

4. In your journal, free-associate about play. For example, some of my associations with play were: happy-go-lucky, jumping, cow jumped over the moon, pop, surprise, and high energy.

5. Laugh as often as possible. Feel the laughter come from the richness of your soul.

Creating Wildness

So, the word wild *here is not used in its modern*
pejorative sense, meaning out of control, but
in its original sense, which means to live a natural life,
one in which the criatura, *creature, has innate*
integrity and healthy boundaries.
Clarissa Pinkola Estés,
Women Who Run With the Wolves

Sometimes while in the thick of writing a book, I find myself acting a bit wild and uninhibited. I find that I am more unpredictable than usual, saying things I would normally edit out. I was recently discussing this with an author of five well-received books, and she said that the same thing happens to her while writing a book. When we free the creative spirit and allow ourselves to take in life deeply, we find in ourselves an innate wildness surfacing and wanting to speak. This same wildness causes children to scream while they play. Even though writing is usually an isolated event, it is something that takes us outside of ourselves into another energy flow. In this way, wildness is cultivated. It wants so much to be with us that it comes in and sets up camp while we are busy writing and being creative. This doesn't mean we have split personalities. We're just playing with our own wild nature, which needs to be cultivated and appreciated in its own unique way.

Running Wild

1. Become wild and natural. Think of something you could do in your everyday life that would serve as a personal statement of your own unique wildness. Ask the angels to help you. They love to encourage natural behavior.

2. Take a deep breath and as you exhale say the word *wild.* Do this and imagine wild energy–energy that isn't tamed or diluted–rushing out with each breath. Get in touch with the wild feeling and write down any thoughts about wildness that come to you while you breathe the energy. Or paint a picture of it, write a song, or just enjoy the feeling without doing anything else. One thing that may happen is that you'll begin to

feel like a particular animal or that a particular type of animal's energy is in touch with you. This can be fun; go with it. Kids naturally play that they are animals, and adults can do this, too. Each of us identifies with a certain animal or two. Think about which animals you feel an affinity to and investigate what they represent in your life. Use your insights in your creative pursuits. Investigate the angelic connection.

3. Play with words and phrases that have *wild* in them: wilderness, walk on the wild side, wildlife, wildcat, wildflower, wild angel, Wild West, and wild you.

4. Read the book *Women Who Run With the Wolves* by Clarissa Pinkola Estés.

Creating Love

Love vibrates rapidly. Fear has a slower rate of vibration. Those who channel fearful energies find that as time passes, the fear vibration grows heavy, depressing. Eventually, it brings sleep, gloominess, discouragement, despair. The love vibration brings enthusiasm, energy, interest, perception. This is what will heal the world: clear and undistorted perception, flowing through a you that is not self-reflective in the egoic sense, but self-reflective in the sense of knowing the God within.

Ken Carey, *Return of the Bird Tribes*

Love is an energy that flows through us from the Creator outward. We cannot withhold love or try to manipulate or control with it. Love is pure divine energy, and if we are willing to allow it to flow through us, it will travel far and wide, with our own divine essence included. Trouble comes when we block a channel for love to come through freely and joyously. Maybe we perceive a good reason for our blocking this channel—a reason we are not able to love—but this is not so. There are no good reasons for blocking love, and if we allow ourselves to be a channel for divine love, we are able to love all. Love is always waiting at the doorway of our heart for an opening to flow through. If we resist, we may feel as if a great pressure is on us. It is difficult to stop the course of a river, and it is difficult to stop the course of love. Don't muddy the waters of love by trudging heavily through life, worrying and blocking love with imagined foes.

Waves of Love Meditation

1. Prepare a quiet moment and do a soften-the-blocks love meditation. Sit quietly and begin to tune into the divine energy of love. Imagine waves of love flowing to earth from the Creator. Imagine a circular pattern to earth, then to heaven, and back again. Stand under a wave and feel it begin to flow through an opening in your soul. Feel the angels crowd around you, protecting you with their colorful love. Is the opening in your heart? Your crown? Your back? Sense where the opening is—it's up to you. Just allow an opening. Is the love flowing out through your hands, heart, head, or eyes? Do you feel the energy getting stuck anywhere? If so, allow information to come to you that will bring you understanding. Release the block and let love with its powerful energy melt the block and transmute its underlying causes. Think of those you love and soften any blocks you feel toward them. Love can reach across any number of miles. It can even touch those who have passed over to other realms.

Allow love to reach into your soul and create smiles, tears, tingles, joy, and blessings. Continue this as long as you like, and keep at it until you feel that your channels for love are clearing. Remember, there is no such thing as conditional love. Conditions (blocks) have nothing to do with love. Love is the highest and most available energy in the universe.

2. Go and love some more!

Creating Prayer

Spend much time in prayer. Prayer is of many kinds,
but of whatever kind, prayer is the linking up of
the soul and mind and heart to God.
Two Listeners, *God Calling,* edited by A. J. Russell

Prayer is a creative way to express yourself to God, the Creator. The kingdom of God is within. To pray creatively, we simply talk to the God within, communicating personally and intimately with our Creator.

Prayer sometimes becomes our only option in certain difficult situations. Many times I find myself in a situation where the only viable action I can take is to pray. When I do so, the situation always turns out for the best. For example, if there is a situation involving another person that is causing me to have negative feelings toward that person and I don't understand exactly why, I know that the best choice is to pray for that person and for the highest good to be done. When you need divine intervention, pray. When you need to have blind faith and require guidance out of the dark, pray. Prayer works. It is a powerful spiritual tool, and it is easy to do.

With the angels in our lives, we have many creative options for prayer. The angels don't want us to pray to them, but they like to help relay our prayers to God. A fun way to pray is to write letters to the angels, seeking higher guidance about a specific issue. Writing letters to the angels can take many forms. You can write a letter to another person's guardian angel asking for divine intervention, or you can write to your own guardian angel with a request to speak to the other person's guardian angel so you can reach understanding on a deeper level. Free will is always respected when the angels are involved, so there is no manipulation.

Norman Vincent Peale talks of a man who had a complete life change through prayer. He writes of him, "He had discovered that prayer is no visionary, pious, mystical exercise for saints and the ultra-devout. He found that it can be a practical method for restimulating the mind which has lost creative skill. And even more than that he found that such praying is an energy-renewing force." Make prayer a creative, energy-renewing force in your life. Prayer brings results and divine guidance. By practicing prayer, you make it a comfortable and welcome part of your everyday life.

Practical Prayer Ideas

1. Ask your angel to join with you as a prayer partner when you are praying for the resolution of a problem. Pray, and then spend time with your guardian angel simply thinking about God. You will feel an energy shift, and your answer will be forthcoming. Look for it in creative ways.

2. Write a prayer request on a card and keep it with you.

Hold the card in your hand whenever you like, at least three times a day, and pray with your angel for creative guidance and the highest good. When you feel you have received an answer, note it on the card, along with any related thoughts, and keep it in a "gratitude file." Creating a prayer box to file the cards in, decorated with angel-related beauty, can be a fun project.

3. When you pray, allow a linking of your mind, soul, and heart to God. If you feel the urge, roar with laughter. Laughter comes straight from your soul. If you feel like crying, your tears will cleanse your mind and soul. Allow love to lift up your heart with joy when you pray. Have an angel experience with your prayer, then let it go.

Creating Faith

The angels' perspective comes from the vastness of infinity and beyond time; from there, they radiate love to everything without judgment.

Dorothy Maclean, *To Honor the Earth*

Many Buddhists believe that most humans on the earth right now are here to work out issues of greed, doubt, hatred, sloth, and agitation. You may agree or disagree with this Buddhist concept, but either way it's good food for thought. Think of the qualities that counteract these issues. What could help with greed? I think that living in the moment without want and truly understanding and knowing "that God alone suffices" is a good solution. Antidotes for hatred include self-love, soul happiness, understanding, and forgiveness. Sloth can be overcome by finding a vocation you enjoy and through action, service, and play. Agitation has to do with our effect on others. If we agitate, we cause anxiety and concern and fan the flames of negative energy. If we are happy without reason, we are mentally at peace and we cannot agitate anyone in this state. Some possible antidotes for doubt are trust, optimism, hope, and faith. Expressing our *creativity* will help with all five issues.

Having faith in angels can be your guiding light. Angels give sight to faith. Instead of blind faith, you receive clear knowing that the highest good is always available to you. With faith, you *know* instead of believe. Faith gives us the will to find the way. Most importantly, when you have faith, you will know in your heart that you are never alone and that you are constantly held in divine love—the angels are with you.

Keeping the Faith With the Angels

1. If you ever get discouraged with the world and question why you should even bother, have faith in your creativity. I find that this saves me every time doom and gloom start to get me down. I think about my own creativity—about the gardens, writings, and art I like to create—and then my world is lighter and brighter and the angels smile. Have faith in your creativity. When all else fails, if you know in your heart that you are creative, you will be okay.

2. Pretend that your angel has a best friend named Faith. Whenever you need faith in a situation, imagine your guardian angel inviting Faith to come by and play with you.

Creating Gratitude

You can clean your aura and raise your vibration by giving thanks. The resonance of gratitude in your body vibrates with your heart center. It allows you to open to receive more.
Sanaya Roman

Gratitude creates a "great attitude." Creating gratitude can be an ongoing meditation you can do all day long. I try to remember to thank everything I encounter. When I am writing on my computer and I have the program do a special function, I thank it when I finish. I thank my car for getting me places. I thank the musicians for the music I listen to. I mentally thank flowers for reminding me of the angels. I thank my cats for being so funny. I thank the water I use to bathe in and drink. I thank the sun for its warmth. I find that when I engage in this process of thanking, I feel happier and lighter throughout the day. I am able to pause and be grateful for the amazing process of life, and this helps me appreciate and be conscious of the angels.

Playing With Gratitude

1. Do your own thanking meditation. No one has to hear you. You can thank things in the privacy of your own mind. Doing this will help you "accentuate the positive and eliminate the negative." Gratitude gives you greater access and attunement to creative energy and makes you aware of the presence of the angels behind every creative breath you take.
2. Go on a nature walk and thank everything you encounter

that reminds you of the goodness of life. Find a stone or a rock and designate it your gratitude reminder.

Creating Flow

We have seen earlier that when an activity is thoroughly engrossing, there is not enough attention left over to allow a person to consider either the past or the future, or any other temporarily irrelevant stimuli.
Mihaly Csikszentmihalyi, *Flow*

Many artists and writers enter an altered state of consciousness when they are creating. When they come back, they are amazed at what they have created. This process is nothing new and unusual; many of us have experienced it. It is an indication of being connected–body, mind, and spirit–to the realm of creative ideas and angelic inspiration. Experiencing this flow is like traveling on the higher ground of our creativity, where we are one with the angels. Flow takes place when we are fully on the earth, yet our minds are connected to heaven. Creating flow entails connecting our energy system with the divine flow of the universe, resulting in a sense of comfort and grace.

Flow comes when we truly enjoy what we are doing. If we feel pressured or on a time limit, flow is more difficult to achieve. If we are obsessed over "serious" details, flow is almost impossible, until we set aside our worries and self-absorption. Do you think that the violin players in a symphony orchestra are worried about what happened in the past or what will happen in the future when they are playing Mozart in the present?

I doubt it. When we truly enjoy doing something we are good at it, flow is present. Flow also helps us to become great at something. Essentially, flow requires attention to the moment, no worries, having the abilities to do what we are doing, and, most important, enjoyment in doing what we are doing. When we enjoy doing something, we are creating joy, and the angels help us.

"Flow Down!"

1. Explaining flow is somewhat ridiculous! So I am going to stop while I feel only slightly ridiculous. Start to notice the flow around you. Watch children play, and allow yourself to experience the flow they create. Ask the angels to help you create flow. Don't get hung up on creating flow. Just ask, and before you know it, you will be experiencing flow. Flow resembles a dreamlike state, and you simply can't create it by thinking about it too much. So ask and be available to experience flow. Each time you experience flow, the next time will come easier. Soon, creating flow will be as simple as breathing.

Creating Focus

I have discovered that I also live in creation's dawn,
The morning stars still sing together,
And the world, not yet half made,
Becomes more beautiful every day.
John Muir

Focus means you have a center to your activities or interests. If you have ever used a camera that didn't have automatic focus, you know that focusing means bringing the picture in as clear as possible. So having focus entails having a clear intention of the picture you want to create. With focus, you have found a certain flavor and bent to your creativity. Having focus and knowing your skills allows you deeper access into the realm of creative inspiration. Focus is like concentration with personal style attached. Focus can also help you get across your main objective; if you have focus, you know what it is you are aiming to create.

Focus is not self-absorption. Focus involves going outside of yourself and standing apart from your moods and personal issues so you can gain clarity. Think about how you can focus the lens of your own creativity. The angels will help, and they may end up becoming an important part of your focus. Examine past creative endeavors and look for your degree of focus and clarity of intention. Also, remember that focus is only one possible component that may help you express your creativity; it is not always necessary. Sometimes you may want to be completely out of focus and see where this state leads you.

Focusing on Heaven

1. When you are out in the world, play a little game with the angels. Every once in a while, stop and focus on heaven. Look around and imagine that you are looking through the angels' lens. What you create in doing this is heightened perception. Colors may look brighter, sounds may change, the air may tingle, and you may see spirit glowing all around you. Bring this heightened perception into your life in whatever way you need, to whatever you are doing whenever you want.

The angels' lens is always available for us to look through. Have fun.

2. Do a focus meditation. Think about a creative endeavor in your life and pretend you have a focusing lens as you examine it. Write about any insights you receive.

Creating Kindness

Be kind, for everyone you meet is fighting a hard battle.
Plato

Kindness exacts a strict discipline, but not for the reasons we may think. Kindness is so pure in its true form that the slightest degree of fake or insincere energy can contaminate it. The psalmist was right who wrote, "Create in me a clean heart, Oh Lord, and renew a steadfast spirit within me" (Psalm 51:10). To create kindness, we must have a clean heart. Being kind means being gentle and considerate in our conduct toward others. To achieve this, we must be centered ourselves and able to view each situation with clarity and look upon it as a chance to be kind in a unique way. The angels teach us that kindness doesn't necessarily mean doing what someone else wants us to do. It doesn't necessarily mean pleasing someone, unless that is the highest choice in the matter and we know it in our heart. Sometimes when we are the kindest, people project the opposite on us, mainly because they wanted more from us, maybe even a piece of our soul, which is not ours to give.

Innocence allows us to keep kindness pure and simple. A state of innocence does not mean being stupid or foolish. It means being harmless and having respect for life. Keep a feeling of inner innocence when you are creating kindness. If you think you've already lost your innocence, know that it may be hiding, but you can find it. Innocence comes from that place in your soul that is peaceful and serene. Start to tap into an inner space of peace and ask the angels to help you respond to life with innocence. Then your actions will be right for you and you will know when something feels right. Remember, be kind to yourself first. If something you encounter looks like a snake and feels like a snake, then for goodness sake, leave it alone, and direct your attention toward other areas where you can express kindness.

Life teaches us to be less harsh
with ourselves and with others.
Goethe

Considering Kindness

1. Do not kill with kindness. Kindness means being considerate, so consider the situation and respect all involved, including yourself. Keep angelic kindness in mind.

2. When your heart is pure, kindness is not an issue; it is a natural angelic response.

3. Don't let your mind judge kindness. Let your heart and your angel be your guide.

4. Simplify your everyday relationships. Allow the angelic winds of heaven to blow between you and another. The winds will keep anything sticky and negative from attaching to your inner core, where peace and serenity reside.

Creating Generosity

Generosity is a willingness to give, to open without philosophical or pious or religious motives, just simply doing what is required at any moment in any situation, not being afraid to receive anything.
Chögyam Trungpa, *Cutting Through Spiritual Materialism*

Being generous has always been very important to me because I have been so blessed in my life that I want to share my blessings with others. However, at times I have been confused about generosity. Until recently, I associated generosity mostly with giving money or some commodity away. But now I think that generosity is much more than giving things away. Generosity is an energy that needs an abundant reserve, and it has to come from a balanced source. You can give the shirt off your back. You can give your last dime away, if you are in the right heart frame. If, however, you are putting yourself and your needs at a lower level of importance, you are not truly being generous. Giving to feel superior or because you think you are superior is not true generosity. Being able to receive generosity can also be tricky.

Being generous is learning to give what is really needed. Most often, what is needed, more than our money or a gift, is our quality time–our wisdom, our willingness to listen, and our love. Giving freely of whatever is required of you in the moment, and doing it without fanfare or strain, is true generosity. Often our presence is required or requested, and we start to think of ways out instead of ways in. Sometimes I spend more energy and time trying to avoid something that I think would take too much of my time when if I would just surrender and be there in the moment, I would spend less time and energy, and the wonderful energy of generosity would prevail.

"Giving In"

1. What does being generous mean to you?
2. How can you surrender in the moment and be generous?
3. Consider the generosity of the angels. What has their generosity meant to you?
4. Think of yourself as a gift. If you are accepted, fine; if not, fine. Be yourself and surrender in the moment. Allow the angels in, and ask for their guidance. In this way, you will start to become a generous spirit, with the angels in your life, without depleting your source.

Creating Mindfulness

If we're really engaged in mindfulness while walking along the path to the village, then we will consider the act of each step we take as an infinite wonder, and a joy will open our hearts like a flower, enabling us to enter the world of reality.
Thich Nhat Hanh, *The Miracle of Mindfulness*

Stop right now and think about what your mind has been full of lately. It is your mind, and you can fill it with whatever you want. Sometimes, though, it seems as if our minds fill themselves up with the very things we are trying to avoid, such as fear, worries, concerns about work, or a sense that we lack something.

Mindfulness entails making choices with the angels in each moment, asking the angels to help us fill our minds with heavenly thoughts and life-affirming creative thoughts. Mindfulness reminds us to stop and pay attention to the miracle of the present moment.

Mindfulness is really a process of being awake and aware and living in the now. Thich Nhat Hanh wrote a book called *The Miracle of Mindfulness,* and I highly recommend it; it is a book that will help you slow down and fill your mind with peace.

"Bells of Remindfulness"

1. Think of little things that can remind you during the day to fill your mind with divine peace. I call these things "my remindfulness bells." When I hear my wind chimes (I have seven wind chimes strategically placed around my house), I always stop and imagine that the angels are playing a heavenly melody. Other reminders for me to stop and relax into the present moment include hearing a bird sing, hearing children laugh or gleefully scream, and watching my cats roam through the tall grass. Sometimes I pick one reminder to practice at various times during the day, for example, looking up at the sky at least once an hour to remind me of peace. I try to stay conscious of this practice all day. Think of some "remindfulness bells" you can designate in your life to remind you gently to fill your mind with God, the angels, and their divine beauty, peace, and hope.

2. Spend time during the day doing things in slow-motion. For example, while washing your hair, slowly reach for the shampoo bottle, slowly squeeze the shampoo into your hand, and watch carefully as it leaves the bottle. Notice all of the colors,

scents, and sensations of washing your hair in slow-motion. Think of other things to do in slow-motion. This is a good way to create mindfulness.

Creating Humility

Humbleness, forgiveness, clarity and love, all the gifts of the spirit, take root and bloom, and you draw to yourself the Universe's greatest gift: human beings with open hearts.
Gary Zukav, *The Seat of the Soul*

Humility is another balancing act that the angels have brought our way. The reason humility requires balance lies in its meaning. To have humility means to have a humble attitude, and the definition of *humble* is having a modest estimate of one's own importance. Here we must ask the angels how to be humble while loving ourselves and feeling appropriately important at the same time. The answer is to beware of excessive pride. Hubris–pride in its utmost–is what brought the archangel Lucifer down. In a candid moment, a well-known and accomplished man once said that his main issue in life was to overcome the limiting effects of pride. When we are prideful, true comedy unfolds, except we are not in on the punch line until we let go and take an honest look at ourselves and how our pride gets us in trouble. Every time I get carried away with my role as a writer and the important message I want to get across, pain comes into my life in some way to teach me humility. The angels teach us humility as gently as possible, unless we are way off track and need a higher level of pain to get our attention.

Gentle or not, the lessons of humility are important. Ultimately, we are in service to the Creator, and we all have important parts to play, but we have to remind ourselves that we are simply humans, as magnificent as that may be. We are spiritual beings here to educate ourselves and have a good time doing so. We don't receive any report cards to wave in front of other people's faces if we do something well.

I am so grateful that I have soaked up so much love in my life. This love has saved me many times from falling on my face. Ultimately, love is what I will take with me from this earth experience–true love. So when I get carried away with myself, I can quickly come back to earth when I realize that I am not any better, higher, or more important than any other person, that I am loved not because of what I accomplish but because of who I am, and that love is the true glory.

Being a humble spirit brings a great bonus in that you attract more love and goodness into your life. To attract the good, you must be authentically humble, meaning you don't think about it. There is much false humility on the earth, that is, people who think they are stooping to be with those below them, or people who use people in a difficult situation for their ego rather than for the good of all. Don't focus on such people, but be aware that all of these expressions of pridefulness exist as a lesson on the importance of humility.

No More Humble Pie

1. Many people begin to attain humility when they are stuck in an addictive situation and finally turn to a Twelve-Step program. In step two of the Twelve Steps, we come to accept

that a power greater than ourselves can restore our sanity. It is clear how this concept leads to a sense of humility. Step seven actually uses the word *humble:* "We humbly asked God to remove our shortcomings." Addiction and pride are strongly linked. To truly recover from an addiction, we need to accept the fact that we are not in control more or less than anyone else, we are not loved by God more or less than anyone else, and we have not been singled out to suffer more or less than anyone else. In other words, we are special but not for the reasons we may think. We are special just in being who we are and in how we show love. Ask the angels to help you ask God to remove your shortcomings. Ask that your lessons in humility be gentle but thorough. Through humility comes true freedom, and you will not understand this truth until you live it.

2. Consider how to be proud but not prideful. It is okay to be proud of ourselves, especially when we make spiritual breakthroughs and leaps in personal growth. The angels are proud of us for these things, too. The problem arises when we judge things as right or wrong. Remember, there are no right or wrong opinions, no true black-and-white answers. While some might argue this on philosophical grounds, please don't take it seriously. When you begin to see that someone else's opinion is simply different from yours—not wrong or something that you have to change—you will not only attain humility but also experience more wisdom and less stress in your life. When you feel your pride is injured, a grudge can last forever. So think of the things in your life that involve being proud and ask the angels for clear insight. Start to be proud of yourself each time you let go of your pride. The angels will help!

Creating From Your Heart

The Divine Voice is not always expressed in words.
It is made known as heart-consciousness.
Two Listeners, *God Calling,* edited by A. J. Russell

A while back, I had a conversation with a man who had published (but didn't write) a little book that had taken off on its own, without promotion other than word of mouth, to become a best-seller—a book that prompted many letters and positive comments. He told me he was searching for another book like this, so that he would have another best-seller, but he was having a very hard time finding anything like it and couldn't figure out why. He asked me why I thought people loved this book so much and why he couldn't find a similar idea so quickly. I told him that the book he published reaches hearts, touches hearts, and talks to hearts. It was written from the heart to teach love. His book entailed true originality because it was written from the heart of someone who was willing to allow his own special brand of love to be expressed to the world. He may find another book that touches hearts, but it, too, will have to be an original. It will have to come from the heart. Copies just don't do it. There is no set formula for writing or doing something that will touch hearts.

To reach another heart, a message must originate from the heart, from love. Paramahansa Yogananda once said, "Love is the silent conversation between two hearts." So to transmit on the heart level, we need to be willing to give out love to the world. And we need to realize that this is not something we can try to do or talk about doing. We either do it, or we don't. We may do it without even realizing it. Trying, advertising, pushing, explaining, convincing, and copying will not allow your heart to sing to another's. Being yourself, transmitting your own special love, being love, allowing others the freedom to receive your love without trying to convince them, and asking the angels for true heart guidance will allow your heart to reach other hearts. "To hearten" means to make a person feel encouraged. This is what your angels want to do–hearten you to express your true heart-self.

Exploring the Heartland

1. Think of all the words and sayings about the heart: Have a heart, heartfelt, heart's content, heart's desire, forever young at heart, heart of the matter, open heart, by heart, change of heart, take to heart, wear one's heart on one's sleeve, heart-to-heart talk, heartwarming, pull on one's heart strings; there are many more. What does the word *heart* mean to you?

2. Think about what touches your own heart and why.

3. How can you cultivate heart in your own creative gifts? Visualize the angels giving your heart wings. How does it feel? How do the angels help hearts reach one another?

Creating for the Glory of the Creator

Each human being has a soul. The journey
toward individual soulhood is what distinguishes the
human kingdom from the animal kingdom,
the vegetable kingdom and the mineral kingdom.
Only the human kingdom has the experience of individual
soulhood. That is why its powers of creation are great.
Gary Zukav, *The Seat of the Soul*

Everything that the angels do is for the glory of the Creator. The angels sing praises to God all day long. The angels praise God with their love and service. You may wonder how they can watch over us and praise God at the same time. You may also wonder how we can be like angels and praise God all day long, in all that we do. It is very simple. All we have to do is do all that we do for the glory of God. This involves intention. It also has to do with creating a pure soul so that no matter what the rest of us is doing, our soul is in alignment with the highest good. The way we make our soul pure is to pay attention. Human life is a sacred experience. It is a gift, a chance for us to consciously choose to use our free will to love God.

One way to make sure that we create for the glory of God is to be of service out of joy, not duty. That is what the Creator wants–service with a joyful heart. Service with stress and strain is not good for you. Think of service as a form of play in its highest form. Think about your life and how you can make almost anything you are doing into service, with joy and playfulness, for the glory of the Creator.

One thing I know deeply is that people who have a solid spiritual foundation, a spiritual center, will always be okay. I don't mean they will always like the cards life deals them, but they will make it through. At the core of their being, they *know* God and the angels, and this knowledge creates a reservoir of strength. Having a spiritual center means that you carry the light of God for those to see who can. You don't hide it or ignore it.

Several times in my life, I have had people think that I had something special going for me that they had missed out on. They tried very hard to figure it out and explain it. Sometimes they would say, "Oh, she is just lucky," or "Well, she had a good upbringing; she got all the breaks," and then they might try to project something negative onto my personality. This is difficult to write about because it is personal and I don't want to paint the wrong picture. I am writing about it here because it may help someone out there gain some understanding about something very simple. I feel fortunate for one main reason: because, at a very young age, I was allowed to cultivate a relationship with God, and I was supported in this by the people who raised me. This really had nothing to do with religion per se. It had more to do with prayer and spiritual contemplation, two things I have done since I can first remember. Prayer and knowing that the light of God is within me have gotten me through every hardship and lesson I have encountered. So that is my truth, one of my main truths at least. If you are wondering how to go about creating your own spiritual center–if you feel you are missing one–all you have to do is make prayer a consistent part of your life in your own special way. Know that when all else fails, if you surrender to the love of God, everything is going to be okay. It may sound simple, but then, why wouldn't it be?

Devotion as Great Love

1. Creating devotion is a way to allow your true spiritual creativity to come out and play with the angels. We are the only ones who can separate ourselves from God, and it is only through illusion that we do so. We are also the only ones who can tell ourselves how to love and devote ourselves to the Creator. Devotion is a great way to stay in close contact and harmony with the angelic realm. Devotion is personal, and it is your choice how to play with it. Begin with simple awareness.

2. "Hosanna" is a cry of adoration for God. When you feel a need to connect with your soul, which is always in the midst of praising and adoring God, make up a chant or little song with "Hosanna" or "hosanna in the highest" in it.

3. Keep in mind that all psychological problems have a spiritual answer. A spiritual life is absolutely necessary for psychological health. The angels hold the spiritual remedy for whatever ails your soul. Ask them, and you will be led to your own spiritual answer.

4. One definition of *enthusiasm* is "being filled with or inspired by God." When we have enthusiasm for something, we have energy for it. God is the energy of love, so when we are enthusiastic, we are filled with love for what we are doing. If you find that you are not filled with love and enthusiasm for what you do each day, particularly in the creative arena, ask the angels for inspiration. They live at the heart of enthusiasm, and are ever ready to bring some our way.

5. Keep your inner light bright and your center strong and spiritual, and stay close to the angels. In this way, you will be a natural creative force for the glory and the light of the Creator.

Closing Thoughts to Part One

It is the nature of a word to reveal what is hidden.
The word that is hidden still sparkles in the darkness
and whispers in the silence. It entices us to pursue it,
to yearn and sigh after it. For it wishes to reveal
to us something about God.
Meister Eckhart

My underlying hope with Part One is that it has helped you begin to develop a sense of courage to actually make creativity a living, breathing, vital part of your human experience. There are many beliefs about creativity and much has been written about the subject. I started out researching much of this material so that I could cover all of the bases. My intuition and inspiration from the angels, however, took me in a different direction. I realized that I don't need to cover and rehash the usual ideas about creativity. Of course, some of my ideas are influenced by what I have read, but reading alone cannot address the heart of the matter. Words are not enough to convey the courage and self-love available for you to develop and live your own creativity. So whatever happens as you read this book, remember that the words are not the important part. The message from the angels is what's essential, and it will resonate with you in your own special way. I have used many words in this book. I like words, but there is something more beyond the words that I want you to discover and know. I don't know what that something will be for each individual. Only you will know, and I, too, will continue to discover what this book has to offer long after it is published.

The angels can see your creative self at all times. They love you and want you to love yourself in full realization of the magnificent creative being that you are. I know this sounds lofty, but it is true. You are magnificently creative, with access to an infinite realm full of creative ideas to develop. In the angels, you have a cheering section always present to urge you on to greatness.

Don't think too much while waiting for the muse. Keep in mind that there is really nothing to worry about. All is well and in divine hands. The world is getting better, not worse.

Gather the courage to throw out every idea you ever had about creativity and start fresh. I used my niece Elizabeth's words to open the book. Many of us have thought, "Oh, children are so creative, and we have grown out of it," and yet Elizabeth at age twelve is telling us that the older we get, the more creative we are. Children are looking at us, and we *are* creative. Allow old ideas about who you think you are, or who you planned to be, to vanish. Let new energy for being an individual free spirit emerge. Become one who is able to connect with the One.

From now on, the muse will hound you, bringing you messages in the most creative of ways–through your dreams, through birds, through the clouds, through small, still voices, and in countless other ways. You will not rest until you heed these messages and make creativity your way of life with the angels.

Part Two
Getting the Mud Off Our Wings

About Part Two

Is a diamond less valuable because it is covered with mud? God sees the changeless beauty of our souls. He knows we are not our mistakes.
Paramahansa Yogananda

Part Two offers ideas for "getting the mud off our wings" so that we aren't weighted down with outmoded beliefs and worries and can fly free. This process helps clear the mud from the light of our souls so that we can express ourselves clearly and brightly. The mud consists of our negative thought patterns and fears, hitch-hikers that we have picked up on our journey through life and that we somehow forgot to let off at their destination. Sometimes these negative elements can block our creativity, and yet creativity is the antidote to negative programs that consume our time. If you are stuck with worries, fears, and the like, think of games to play with the angels to promote creative ways to change the energy. When I really get stuck with worries and misperceptions, the best way I've found to get rid of them quickly is to just start writing about them with the angels nearby. I do this in a stream-of-consciousness writing style, a practice I share in this section.

Another great way to change perceptions is to do something creative and concrete, such as cooking a meal, rearranging your furniture, drawing a picture, talking to a child, or taking a creative nap with the angels. You will find that your energy system changes gears and shifts to a higher space. When you go back to the original problem, it will seem lighter and you will be more detached from it. You will then be free to stretch your wings and fly!

Chapter 3
Releasing Blocks

We all have issues in our lives that require some creative attention or they will block us and make life less enjoyable. If we ignore our issues and try to go on as if everything was great, we create denial. This denial reaches us on another level and starts to drain our creative energy. Of course, all issues have their own time to be resolved, and this process may take time. So don't try to jump in and blast out problems in an instant. This won't work and just fuels our denial. Think of solving problems as a creative process that will change and expand, ebb and flow. Don't accept explanations that don't resonate with you. Pain is complex and takes a unique face for each of us. In other words, there are really no ready-made answers to solve all our problems. Nevertheless, using our blessed imagination and receiving spiritual guidance from the angels can only help.

Issues can propel us toward creative acts if we will allow ourselves to be open to growth, change, and, most important, spiritual help. Spiritual help is available for every problem, large and small, as well as for every joy in life. When we choose to know God and the angels as a function of everyday life, we will realize that the angels are spiritual helpers, and they can help us in very practical ways. The angels are always there for us, and they can assist us in creative ways when we move toward what is positive. Angels guide us in the direction that will give us the most strength and will most build our character.

When it comes to moving through blocks, *release* is the magic word.

Questioning the Myths of Creativity

1. Being creative means being yourself, freeing your spirit, and feeding your soul. Ask yourself the following questions about creativity, art, and various ways we express ourselves. This process will help give you an idea of beliefs you may hold about self-expression. Remember, there are no good or bad beliefs here; this is a matter of identifying thoughts you have now. Remember to answer questions with your own deepest thoughts and feelings, not by how you may have been taught or by something you read somewhere.

- What does being creative mean?
- What constitutes a creative person?
- What is creativity?
- What is talent?
- What is art?
- Can a successful "fine arts" painter be a talented writer?
- Does every musician or music student need to study scales in order to play the piano well?
- Could a sensitive poet excel in the business world?
- Are all writers former "A students" in English?
- Do you have to be born with talent in order to be an artist?
- After a certain age, is it too late to start developing an art form?
- Should all artists be able to draw, or reproduce, an exact replica of a "still life"?

2. Within each of these questions is a myth about creativity and artistic nature. Look at each question and identify the myth and ask yourself if you at one time (or now) were influenced by it. Think of some more myths you may know of and think about whether these ideas have blocked you in any way. If you find a myth you subscribe to and want to change this, play with the "Declaration of Independence" on pages 102–3.

Freeing Your Creative Voice

Sometimes I am asked, "When did you first know you wanted to be a writer?" I never really thought about whether I wanted to be a writer. It simply never occurred to me that I wasn't. I have been a writer for a long time. I can't claim that all the writing I have done comes anything close to literary excellence. That hasn't been my goal. I started keeping a diary at a young age. It was a five-year diary with a little space to write each day, so mostly I listed my activities for the day. Quite often, I added my feelings or a commentary on life. Things were so simple then but seemed so crucial. Then there were the silly times in junior high, such as when my friend and I rewrote our school newspaper with our own illustrations and our own special departments. Another writing exercise in junior high – not one the teachers assigned – were those long notes my friends and I would write to one another, sometimes during class and sometimes at home, where we expressed our feelings about everything from boyfriends to what we had for dinner the night before. In high school came my first real journal. I bought a blank book with a black cover and a picture of a person sitting on some rocks by the ocean at sunset, with a caption that read, "Thought Is Free." This is when I became

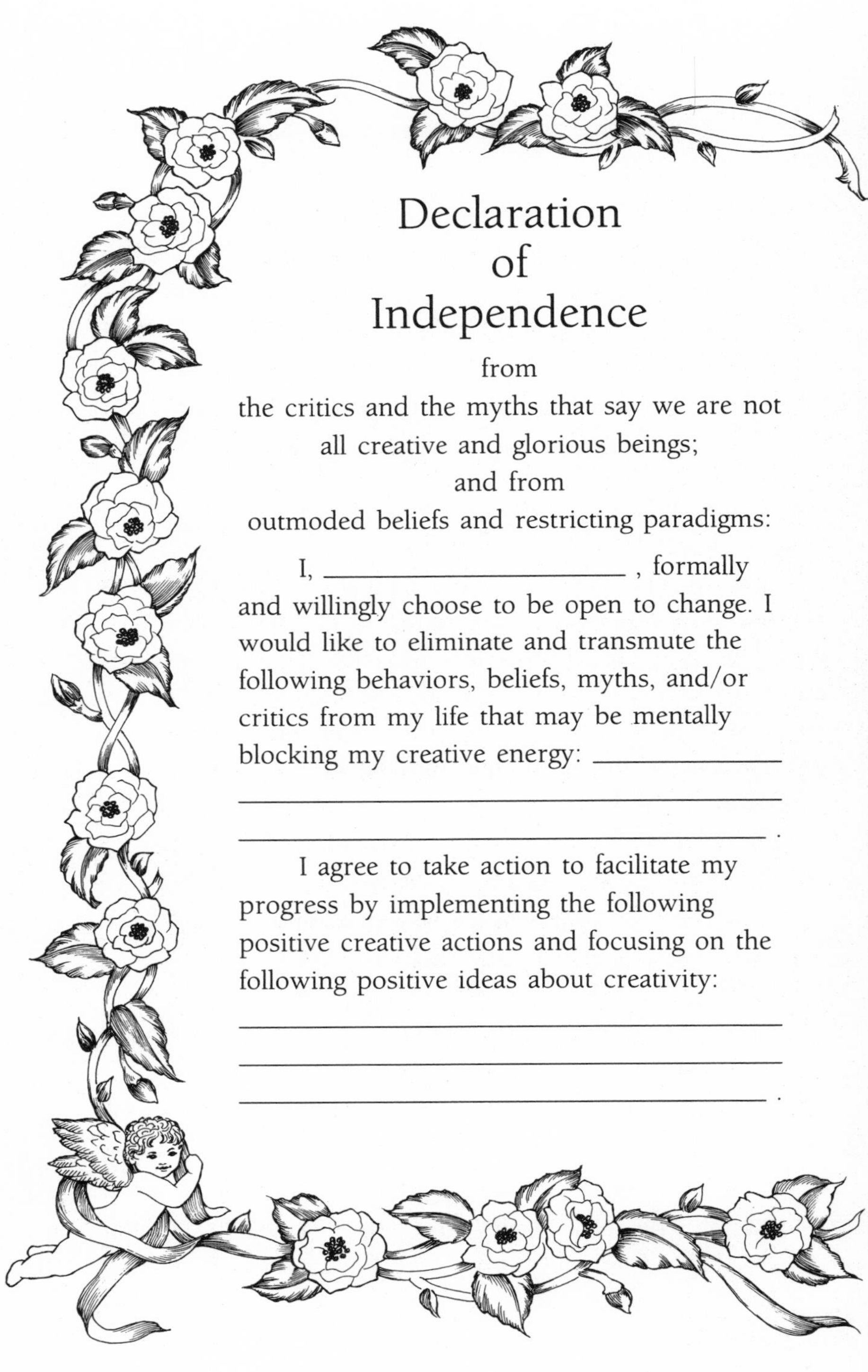

Declaration of Independence

from
the critics and the myths that say we are not all creative and glorious beings;
and from
outmoded beliefs and restricting paradigms:

I, ______________________ , formally and willingly choose to be open to change. I would like to eliminate and transmute the following behaviors, beliefs, myths, and/or critics from my life that may be mentally blocking my creative energy: ____________

____

____ .

I agree to take action to facilitate my progress by implementing the following positive creative actions and focusing on the following positive ideas about creativity:

____

____

____ .

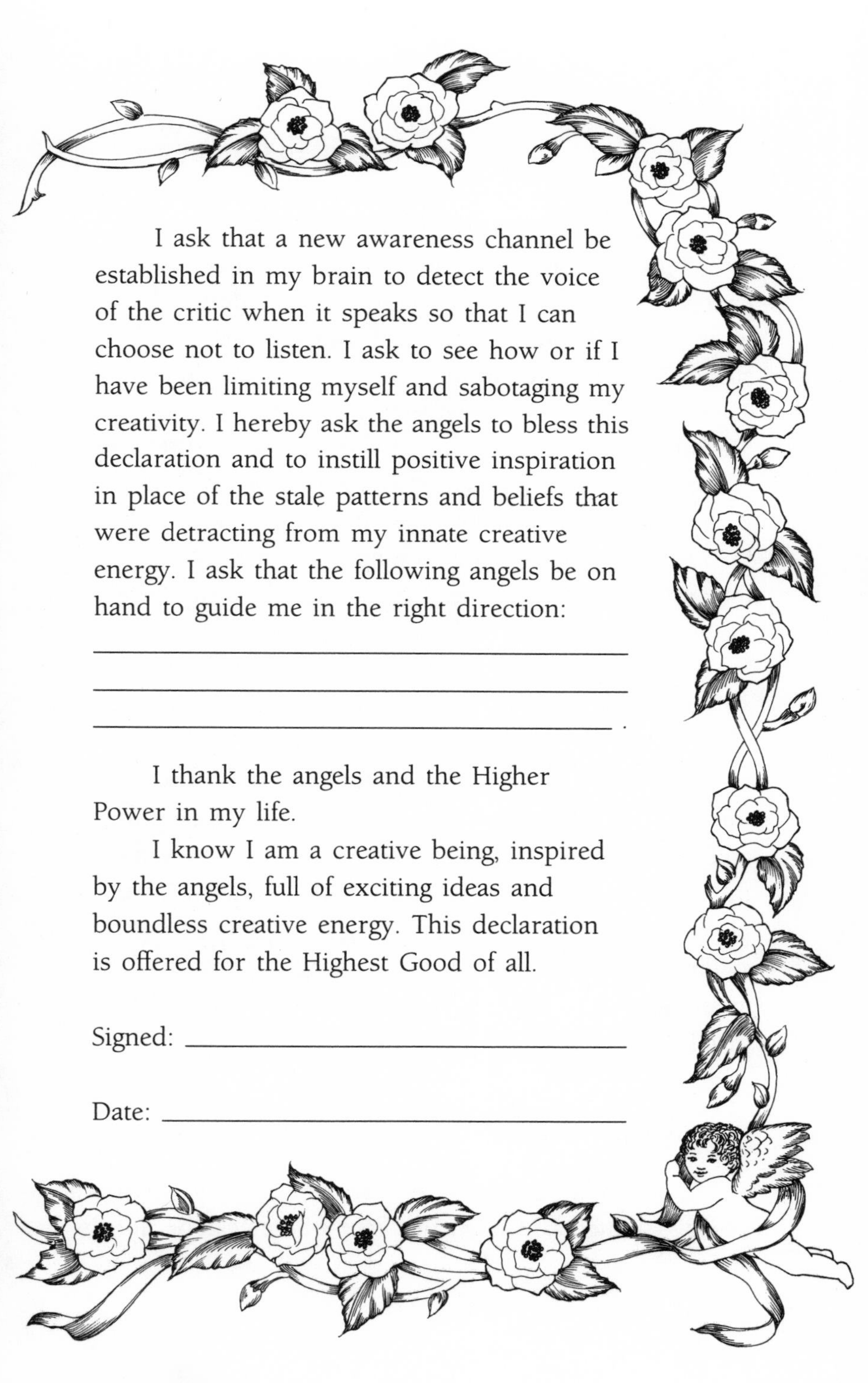

I ask that a new awareness channel be established in my brain to detect the voice of the critic when it speaks so that I can choose not to listen. I ask to see how or if I have been limiting myself and sabotaging my creativity. I hereby ask the angels to bless this declaration and to instill positive inspiration in place of the stale patterns and beliefs that were detracting from my innate creative energy. I ask that the following angels be on hand to guide me in the right direction:

____

____

___________________________________.

I thank the angels and the Higher Power in my life.

I know I am a creative being, inspired by the angels, full of exciting ideas and boundless creative energy. This declaration is offered for the Highest Good of all.

Signed: ______________________________

Date: _______________________________

a writer in my own way. This was sacred time for me. I could write about my feelings, I could write poetry, I could act silly or serious, and no one could restrict my spirit.

Writing is personal. Some people have unique talents that express literary genius, while others promote ideas with a unique twist, yet their writing may not win awards. Other writers weave stories that stir your feelings through the simplest of words. There are many kinds of writing, and I believe we are all capable of being writers if we have the desire and can set aside restrictions and limiting beliefs that may keep us from actually putting the words down on paper. Remember, most readers read for ideas; that is, they are looking for something to stimulate thought. Only a few people read with a totally critical eye on the writing and structure itself, and quite often these people miss the ideas and inspiration. One more thought: Consider being an author versus being a writer. An author is an originator of ideas, bringing new light to ideas.

The first writing exercise I want to share with you is something that will allow you to get in touch with your writing voice and make the process fun. It is also a way to begin writing with the angels and discovering yourself as a creative writer. This particular exercise was inspired by an English homework assignment given in my first year at college. A version of this exercise can also be found in *Guardians of Hope*. This is an exercise in following the stream of consciousness.

Defining the Moment

1. Sometimes when I am clouded over by worries and negative thoughts, I find a quiet spot where I can be alone with

myself and the angels, get my journal out, and start writing about it. I write down everything and anything that is happening right now, including my worries, fears, and happy thoughts; the temperature of the room and how it affects me; what is happening outside the window if I am inside the house; the sounds I hear, what it smells like; and how the light is playing in the room or outside. I write about how tired, nervous, tense, relaxed, or numb my body feels. In other words, I try to define my entire experience in the now, including all of the things that take me out of the now, such as worries.

By writing all this down with freedom, you will discover many interesting things. One, you may discover you shift from happy thoughts to sad or uncomfortable thoughts very quickly. You are not necessarily frozen in any one mood, as we are sometimes led to believe. Two, you may uncover the very essence of what is worrying you and then you can begin to brainstorm on possible solutions or alternate scenarios. Three, if you allow your mind to wander completely, strange thoughts may come to the surface (write them down), and the memory of places will surface for no apparent reason.

Keep recording your experience of the now. Define in some loose way all the sensations your senses are experiencing, and abandon rules. Go wherever your mind desires. Follow any stream of consciousness you choose. Go where it leads, then veer off in your own direction until you discover another stream. Follow whatever voice comes forth, and always remember you are in charge. Have arguments with these voices if you choose; dialogue with the world. Try to keep your hand moving the whole time. Don't stop to think; think on the paper.

2. If you enjoy this stream-of-consciousness exercise, you

may want to do a short version of it every morning or some other time every day. I try to do this exercise often. I just get out my journal while I am still in bed, drinking my coffee, and follow my stream of consciousness. I don't make a big deal out of it, but it is a fun way to wake up and clear my mind and also to see what I could constructively focus on (or not focus on) during the day. This practice is also beneficial for learning to go off into another realm or level of consciousness when you write.

3. Another practice I do in my writings I call "Random Thoughts." By titling this practice "Random Thoughts," I allow myself to put forth thoughts and ideas I have that don't really need to be connected to anything. Usually I pick a theme and then randomly philosophize on it. Pick a subject and give yourself permission to think randomly and philosophize. This is a good way to come up with ideas to support a writing project or other creative venture.

Creative by Mistake

The same ground on which you fall can be used
as a support to help you get up again, if you
learn from your experiences.
Paramahansa Yogananda

Have you been allowed to make mistakes in your life? Do you allow yourself to make mistakes? Many amazing creative discoveries have come about through mistakes. What is a mistake really? The dictionary says that it is something done incorrectly or an incorrect idea or opinion. Well, who is the one deciding what is incorrect or wrong with an idea or opinion? If there are no accidents, then there are no mistakes. Be easier on yourself when you feel you have "mis-taken" something. A way around this is to just be careful – "care-full," not "care-less." Being careful means asking for direction from your inner guidance and the angels. Being careful is also being aware of the present and what the present requires for your highest action.

To express our truths, we sometimes have to take a risk and go into the unknown. Sometimes the unknown is uncomfortable and feels like a big mistake. The angels will help you with risk taking, and it won't seem so risky if you know the angels are with you and that everything is going to be okay. Our expectations are what give us the most trouble in the area of risk taking. Usually we go into the unknown with expectations; yet how can we expect something we don't know? "Cease expecting, and you will gain all things" is true here. You will always gain and learn, and you don't need to put limitations on anything by expecting to learn a certain thing or expecting a certain outcome. Next time you think you have made a mistake, get your angel sight out and look for the creativity.

Critics: The Gestapo of Creative Expression

Loyalty to a petrified opinion never yet broke
a chain or freed a human soul.
Mark Twain

The inner critic can resemble an actual person or a voice that speaks to you in your mind, giving opinions and finding faults – imperfections – in your personality and in your creative expression. It strikes me as odd that critics even exist in the external world, especially movie and art critics, because the criticism they expound is simply based on their own opinions, so why would the rest of us get attached to someone else's opinions? Quite often I see a movie that has received bad reviews, and I absolutely enjoy it. I also find it strange when critics tell us what they would have done differently with an art form. Critics are usually those who don't create themselves, but wish they could, yet they have the nerve to think they could do it better. The point is that critics are simply giving their opinions, and others are listening and taking stock.

The true danger comes when our own personal critics give their opinions in our minds. Then we take stock and block our own self-expression. Awareness equals choice, and choice equals change. So the bottom line of this self-exploration is simply to achieve awareness.

Who Are Your Critics?

1. Sometimes we have our own personal critics in the external world, present in the form of girlfriends, boyfriends, parents, or even strangers who are simply out in the world somewhere disapproving of our life-styles. These people may not even know we regard them this way, but every time we do something creative we are overshadowed with personal thoughts, such as, "No, I'd better not say or do that–so and so wouldn't like it," or "This may not sound intelligent enough; people will think I am stupid." Make a list of your personal critics, if you have any. Ask yourself some questions about them:

- Is there anything you would like to say to these critics?
- Is there anything you are trying to prove to them?
- When did you first notice them in your consciousness?
- Do you compare yourself to them or do they compare you to others in your mind? If so, how and to whom are you compared?
- What do these critics really represent in your life?
- Could you be a critic for someone else? If you answer yes, explain who and why.
- What is a critic?
- Can you avoid these critics or eliminate them completely from your consciousness? If not, can you find a way to transmute their negative influence?

2. Write about your overall feelings about this subject. Tell the angels all about the critics who live in your mind. If you feel you have never had a free space to express yourself, this practice can be very important for your spiritual and personal growth.

3. Sometimes we are so affected by our critics that they take up residence in our bodies. They may remind us they are there with a stiff neck, an ulcer, a headache, or a feeling of fatigue. Start to think of these critics as fiction and allow them to leave peacefully. Write an eviction notice to them. Do whatever you can to get them out of your body.

4. The angels can help you with these critics. You can ask the angels to help you create a boundary of light around you that the critical voice cannot cross. If you have human critics, you can ask the angels to speak to their angels and give them something to like instead of to criticize. You can ask the angels

to give you deeper insight into what is really going on with these critics, and the angels will also let you have some fun with the critics.

5. Listen to your angel cheerleaders. They are always cheering for you, and if you tune in to them you will receive a positive message about how wonderfully creative and great you are! The next exercise will also help you get the critics out of your mind and body.

Giving Yourself a Case of "Don't Know Mind"

So many times in our lives, we fantasize about what people are thinking, doing, and saying when we are not around. Often we start to confuse our fantasies and think that we know the truth about what is really going on. Then, if we don't like our fantasies, we drive ourselves crazy trying to control the perceptions, thoughts, and actions of the world around us when we aren't present. (By the way, this is impossible.) The best way to get rid of this control issue is to become more mindful of the moment. We only really "know" the moment, and sometimes in the moment we are off in the future or past worrying about how to control things that have already happened or that have yet to happen.

"Don't Know Mind"

1. Think of something that is bothering you, and surrender to the moment by accepting that you "don't know" (and probably don't want to know). Start saying to yourself during the day, "I don't know, I don't know." Allow a feeling of peace to take

over each time you say or think "I don't know." Say to the angels, "Angels, I just don't know." The angels do know. Let them guide you to true knowing. True knowing does not involve very much information. Free yourself from the need for information. "Don't Know Mind" is modeled on a Zen practice that allows our original nature, or natural mind, to exist and flourish.

2. Finish the sentences:

- I don't know . . .
- I don't know . . .
- The angels know . . .

"Don't Know Mind" will free you if you realize that all you have is the moment, and the rest is all "don't know stuff." Since we don't really know, we may as well have a positive experience of what we don't know. We have the choice.

What's the Problem?

When we're facing a problem, first, of course, we benefit from asking the angels to help us accept ourselves and our present situation fully. Then we can look at the issues we have labeled problems. What exactly *is* a "problem"? Why do we struggle and become frustrated when one enters our life? Basically, I enjoy a challenge, so I ask myself, "Why don't I enjoy this problem?" Well, the reason is that I attach myself to the problem and then fear that it will have some sort of negative effect on my life. When I look at patterns in my life, especially since bringing the angels into my life, I see that everything works out for the best and I always solve the problems and I gain wisdom from them. So I really have no need to fear problems. In fact,

I am working on welcoming them as a simple exercise in living, as simple as a basic math problem in a child's workbook. I am forgiving myself for having struggles because this is part of being human.

Problems

1. Make a problem list. Simply list your problems and struggles. Don't add solutions now or any other thoughts. Wait for a few days, weeks, or months. Then come back and look at the problems on the list. Add any pertinent information, such as how these problems were solved or if they're still current. If there are any problems you would like the angels to take back to the universal recycling plant, declare them, in writing, "property of the universe." Date the problem list so you can add more at other times.

2. Another simple thing to do when you have a problem is to say to yourself, "This is not a problem," or "This is not my problem," whenever the thought or problem comes into your mind during your waking hours. Declare with the angels that something is not a problem. List the problem and then after it write, "This is not a problem."

Keeping a Sense of Humor

Sometimes I think that my sense of humor has a mind of its own. When I am feeling overwhelmed with the world, I end up resisting its urges to lighten up and have fun in the moment. I've found the following process helpful in overcoming this tendency toward heaviness: I ask my sense of humor, "What is so funny about this?" Then I wait for an answer. Usually, just stopping and thinking about humor can change a situation for the better—and the lighter.

What's So Funny?

1. Have an argument with your sense of humor about why something is so serious and should not be taken lightly and why it has to bring pain. Hopefully this will lead to laughter.

2. Another way to do this practice is to argue with your guardian angel about why something is so serious and awful. Have a dialogue with your guardian angel on the merits of taking things seriously (clue: there really aren't any merits) and have fun with it. Write your dialogue if you want to have a good laugh in the future when you read back over it.

Dealing With Your Shadow

In *Guardians of Hope,* I entitled one chapter "Reckoning With Your Shadow." All of us have a dark side—the shadow cast from the light. For a loose definition, we could say that the dark side of our personality is the side we often want to hide from the world.

Don't Be Afraid of the Dark

1. Think about your shadow. In a world of light, there are always shadows, but the slightest repositioning sheds light onto the place the shadow was covering. You may want to draw your shadow and list the things hiding in it. You may not know

anything about your shadow. Use this as a discovery exercise. Without preconceived knowledge, use your imagination and pretend you know everything about your shadow and write about it.

2. A key idea to remember as you explore your shadow is that the angels are light and will help you illuminate the dark corners of your mind. They will allow you to see it in their light–their nonserious light.

Discovering Optimism

Having many worries can be very draining. If there are worries in your life, there are also creative solutions and positive outcomes to have faith in. If you are worrying too much, it may be that you expect a negative outcome or that you are trying to control a situation that you really have no control over. Remember, we only really have control over our own reactions and responses to life, and sometimes we may feel these control us rather than the other way around. If you have worries, take the time to deal with them and change them to a guiding factor for trusting in the goodness and order in the universe. The angels can help you come up with the faith and trust to change all worries into creative thinking for the advancement of optimism.

Don't Worry–Think Creatively!

1. An easy way to transform worry is to change it to "creative thinking to encourage problem solving" and to give yourself a limited time to do it in. Get your journal out and start to worry. By this I mean to think creatively about your problems. Write whatever you want to about your present worries

until you feel you have sufficiently covered the subject. Keep a feeling of detachment in the air. If this is difficult, ask the angels to help you.

2. After you have finished your "worrying," tell yourself you cannot think about these worries for another twenty-four hours. Then, after twenty-four hours, reread your worries and write down your insights and worry some more if you need to. If you find that during the day you just can't stop worrying, go back to this page and write about it. Begin to look for core anxieties and basic fears that lurk within your worries. Note any patterns or reoccurrences.

"Not Bad"

I hear the word *bad* used far too often. I use it occasionally. This is a word I personally enjoy doing battle with. I think it is used as a wastebasket label when other words could describe what we mean in a clearer, more descriptive way, which would help us get past the negative commitment we make when we decide something is "bad." Judgments and labels also promote polarization, which tends to confuse issues for us humans, because there are no real black-and-white issues. We can begin to deal with labels and judgments in a constructive way by noticing patterns we may want to change and asking the angels for assistance and awareness. Awareness allows us the choice to change.

"Bad" Company

1. Make a list of "bad things" in your life or that you see in the world. Go over your list and pick a new word instead

of *bad* to describe the list. For example, some synonyms for bad are unpleasant, hurtful, serious, wicked, severe, evil, vile, wrong, abandoned, vicious, disgusting, false, terrible, and rotten. Or, find new words that are not necessarily synonyms for "bad."

2. Now describe your experience or perception of each "bad" thing on your list and then explain how it affects you personally. If anything positive could come from this bad thing, state it. There are ways to describe bad things that can cancel out their intrinsic badness. How would the angels describe these bad things? Use this exercise as an expansion tool, expanding your perception of issues so that you are not so closely attached to anything being "bad."

Suffering Is Not a Virtue!

In the history of human spirituality, one can find many cases of people suffering as a way to know God. I don't mean basic, everyday suffering. Historically, such people endured hard suffering, and it did bring them closer to God. Well, that was then and this is now. Times have changed, and it is no longer necessary to suffer as a way to know God and gain favor. Of course, you have a choice, and if you want to suffer of course you can. I have found, however, that joy, happiness, and laughter bring me closer to God. If you also find that joy brings you closer to God than suffering, you are probably interested in finding new ways to transmute the suffering in your life and encourage joy. There is also a secret that is hard for us to grasp: You can be happy and be in a state of pain at the same time. When I mean is that at those times when there is pain in our lives (physical or mental), we don't have to commit to a downward spiral of suffering or think that we can't laugh one minute and cry the next.

Humans are allowed to have more than one feeling at a time and to change our perceptions of a situation whenever we want. We don't have to be in a bad mood for a certain length of time or wait until something magically comes along and changes it all. We also don't need to punish ourselves if we made a "mistake" or something happened in our lives that temporarily sent us in what appeared to be a direction away from God. We can change anything by letting go of our one-sighted way of thinking and labeling. It is all about just being free in the moment.

Suffering Is Relative

1. Explore your own suffering and unhappiness by answering the following questions.

- What is making you suffer?
- How can the angels help?
- What do you expect from your suffering?

2. Explore the idea that to transmute and change the negative impact of a state of suffering is to be so familiar with it that it is no longer an issue. You can easily transcend something that brings suffering once you understand and acknowledge it—not deny that it exists. This goes for any aspect of your personality you feel you have to change or remove. Begin to live with it and understand the full reason it exists, and the aspect will turn into an embellishment that will add character to your personality. Write about it.

Free to Explore

Free spirits enhance humanity in the most colorful way; broken spirits dull humanity. Peace and spirituality do not equal boring. Losing your ego does not mean losing your personality. Taming does not have to mean breaking or damaging. Has your spirit been damaged in any way? Have your wings been caught in a snag or, worse yet, clipped? No matter where you are physically, your mind is always free to explore.

Free Spirit

1. Write about your spirit. Has it been gently tamed or broken and forced into confinement? What can you do to allow it to soar without spinning out of control?
2. Ask your angels to help you with this; it is important. The angels want you to be a free spirit who will help them promote love and beauty on earth.

Our Worst Fears

Sometimes our worst fears do happen, but I know one truth: They only happen when we can handle them. When we predestine a fear and give it power before it happens, we will suffer many times longer than if we surrender and allow our inner resources to help us cope, grow, and go on with our lives. As we trust and keep it light, we are protected and never alone. We create isolation by attaching to thoughts of the past or future. We can keep in mind that our bodies sometimes have difficulty knowing what is imagined and what is real. In other words, fear of a future event can mean stress for the body now. The following exercise can help you transform your fears.

Fear Busting

1. Write a story about your worst-fear scenario. Allow yourself total freedom and courage to delve deeply into your worst fear. Give yourself permission to be morbid or outrageous (think of Stephen King!). Ask the angels to protect you and declare that you are writing about fear to help transcend it and transmute it. In other words, you are not letting yourself be ruled by your fears, because you know fear can cloud your creative vision and keep you from forging new paths of light for others to follow.

2. Now rewrite the story. Have fun, and give it a happy ending. You can write in the third person if you like, or, if you don't have a worst-fear scenario, you can make one up or write about one from the past for insight into what you may be denying. Don't do this exercise unless you want to be free yourself from a fear and are willing to break through some old beliefs or barriers, with the result being new thinking and perceptions. Once upon a time . . .

Ambition, Prosperity, and Manipulation

To achieve greatness,
you must be willing to surrender ambition.
Carol Osborn, *Spiritual Principles of Life-Driven Business*

To prosper means to thrive successfully. *Ambition* means an eager or inordinate desire for honor, superiority, power, or attainment, and *ambitious* means strongly desirous. *Manipulation* means to control the action of, to manage artfully or fraudulently, or to adjust to suit one's purposes.

To thrive successfully, prosper, or grow well, we need clarity and purity of intention. Can we have clarity and pure intentions if we are strongly desirous of something (ambitious)? Are we in a position to allow life to just flow along, accepting ourselves and others, if we are constantly trying to adjust situations to suit our own purposes (manipulation)? I don't think so. In our society, we are taught at a very young age to manipulate our world to get what we want. This seems to be a natural drive. When we are young, we usually find ways to manipulate the world around us. We may even think it is cute (it usually is) when little children beg us and make deals to get some candy or a toy. It is possible that many of us have been positively reinforced, at some point in our growth, for manipulating our world and the people in it.

Then we hear about the merits of ambition. "If you want to get somewhere, you had better be ambitious," which means we had better strongly desire power and authority. What is wrong with this picture spiritually?

If we manipulate, we bring trouble and unrest to ourselves and those around us. Manipulating is like saying "my will be done" by any means it takes. If we disturb the balance or the flow of life, it will be restored one way or another. So look into your life and ask yourself if you are trying to manipulate something, someone, or sometime. Let go of it. Lurking at the core of manipulation is desperation and hopelessness. If something in your life is causing you despair, examine it for signs of manipulation. Manipulation and ambition go against the grain of angel prosperity.

True prosperity is the result of being mentally peaceful in your everyday life. Can you be at peace and be obsessed with pushing the river? Not likely. When we are at peace, we don't have the desire to control other people or situations. A peaceful, happy, and centered person attracts abundance that is not dependent on outward situations involving people or things. Peace of mind is the magic ingredient that helps us thrive successfully.

When we discuss prosperity, of course, the issue of money often arises. This is a consistent issue in most of our lives regardless of how much or how little we have. All we can do is our best in each moment. We can do what our hearts tell us and never blame ourselves for any lack in our lives. Everything is temporary, changing, up and down, back and forth. Stay true to your heart. The angels want you to keep love, hope, joy and laughter alive on this planet. They are asking this of you because it is very important now to have hope and live in the moment. Don't torment yourself over debts and money issues.

Balancing Your Act

1. To stop manipulating and to achieve great happiness, don't be "driven" by your goals. Be fully alive in each moment, then you won't need to be "trying to make it." Trying means not doing, so being is the goal, and that takes place when we are at peace with the moment.

2. If you strongly desire something, look at what is really motivating you. What do you expect to get when you achieve that which you strongly desire? Sometimes we are not even

aware of what is truly motivating us. Think of ways you can surrender your desires to get what you want.

Closing Thoughts to Chapter 3

Mary, Queen of the Angels, relayed this
message to the visionaries at Medjugore:
If you want to be very happy, live a simple life,
humble, pray a lot, and don't worry and fret over
your problems—let them be settled by God. Don't
think about wars, chastisements, evil. It is when
you concentrate on these things that you are
on the way to enter them. Your responsibility
is to accept divine peace, to live it.
Father Guy Girard, Father Armand Girard, and Father
Janko Bubalo, *Mary, Queen of Peace, Stay With Us*

Before ending this chapter, I have some closing ideas to impart: Be less self-absorbed and much more moment-absorbed. Practice going beyond tormenting yourself by analyzing too much or thinking about yourself too much. Don't get stuck in the mud of labels and judgments. Live a spiritual life. Use your innate creative energy wisely.

Begin to release the idea that life should be free of "struggle." *Struggle* is defined in the dictionary as "making a vigorous effort under difficulties; a hard contest; overcoming an opponent or problem." You have probably heard the statement "It's always *something*" in reference to life. The "something" in this statement means a new problem or opponent to face. Well, I'm afraid this is true. No matter what, no matter how enlightened we get, no matter how wise we become, the truth is there is always "something" we must overcome or tackle. Life is education, and with education come lessons and practice and research and study. If we know that there will always be something to learn about and deal with concerning our human existence on this planet, then why work on getting rid of struggles when they will be there anyway? In other words, why waste the energy "trying" to live without problems when "problems" are a daily part of our earthly experience? Here is the key: We can change that which we know we have the power to change, and what we have the power to change is our perception and attitude toward something.

When we concentrate on eliminating our problems (such as debts, relationship troubles, basic survival issues), we start to identify ourselves with the problems. You are not your debts; you are not your troubles. You are you. When we think about our problems all the time and start to identify ourselves with them, we do ourselves a great injustice. Another situation resulting from too much energy spent trying to eliminate our struggles is that we begin to live in the future: "I'll be okay as soon as I get that check." "Everything will be fine when I find my true love." Well, everything is okay now. When we use the bulk of our energy toward a commitment to living in the present, in full acceptance of ourselves and our place in the universe now, then the miracle of happiness without reason has a chance to unfold.

I find that as I accept the idea that life has its struggles and I welcome problems as a chance to learn more about living in a positive state of mind, my life runs more smoothly. These days I give over to the angels my wonderful problems as I tire of them. They don't mind. I also imagine what these "problems" look like to the angels, since they can't possibly take them seriously. When they give me a glimpse of their perception, I have to laugh, because it is all so funny and preposterous!

Chapter 4

Angelic Expressionism

For someone who has grown in evolution to the point that she or he understands that this precious birth is an opportunity to awaken, is an opportunity to know and perhaps to be God, all of life becomes an instrument for getting there: marriage, family, job, play, travel—all of it.

Ram Dass, *Grist for the Mill*

Expressionism is a style of writing, painting, drama, or music seeking to express the artist or writer's emotional experience rather than represent the physical world realistically. Angelic expressionism seeks to express the spiritual experience of everyday life in angelic colors. The imagination is where we meet and nourish our soul. There is a spiritual artist within your soul waiting to express the beauty and depth of being human. Your guardian angel knows this artist well and wants to help inspirit this artist out into the open so you will know her or him well. The angels want your whole life, your everyday life, to be a practice of the art of being creative and happy. Angelic expressionism will encourage this.

One gift the angels have brought to my life is the realization that spirituality is an everyday thing. It is not something that needs to take us away from ourselves, our personalities, and our daily lives. We can be just who we are when we came into this life and understand the spirituality that exists in our own backyard. If we were born into a particular religion, we can explore this religion with the angels in a deeper way. Most often, this will enrich our lives with more meaning than going outside the familiar. Instead of becoming ascetic, we can become aesthetic and increase the beautiful pleasing qualities of our lives for a deeper experience of the divine. We have many spiritually creative choices to make with the angels in our lives. When we express who we are in everyday life, we are on the way toward creating authentic living.

Often we humans seem to want spiritual experience to be supernatural, to take us to other realms, but we are here on the earth right now for a specific purpose (to have fun), and it is important that we fully experience the here and now, the everyday acts of doing the dishes, caring for our community, and enjoying our jobs. I find it a fun irony that when the angels, who spend their time in another realm, came into my life, I realized for the first time the true importance of my being in this earth realm fully, as a spiritual being having a human experience.

To begin with, I am going to help you, once and for all, get past any doubts you have that it is okay to be and admit that you are creative. I am taking creative license to offer you an actual license issued by your guardian angel, sanctioned by the Creator, witnessed by me. Your very own creative license!

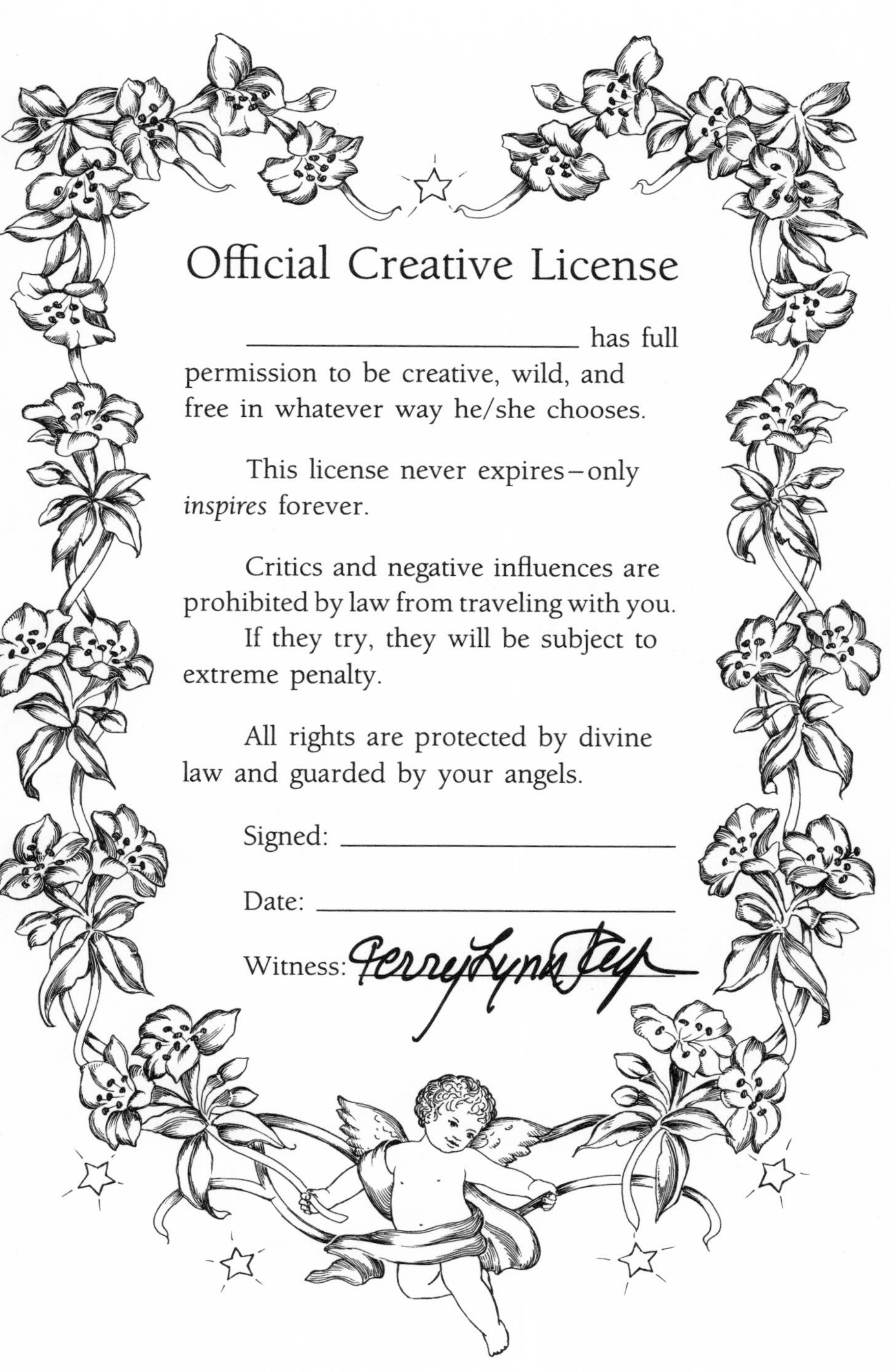

Official Creative License

______________________ has full permission to be creative, wild, and free in whatever way he/she chooses.

This license never expires—only *inspires* forever.

Critics and negative influences are prohibited by law from traveling with you. If they try, they will be subject to extreme penalty.

All rights are protected by divine law and guarded by your angels.

Signed: ______________________

Date: ______________________

Witness: ______________________

Whole Self-Expression

[W]e are both earthly beings, with our feet on the ground, and beings of inspiration and imagination and weightlessness. We're both. That's our genius, and we must not be talked out of it.
M. C. Richards

I'd like to share some feelings about what I feel that our soul is. The soul is our creative imprint from God. Our soul does not need words to understand meaning, and our soul is in constant contact with God and the angels. Our soul responds to harmonic resonance and beauty. Our imagination is our direct link into our soul and also our direct connection to the angelic realm. Never believe that imagination is not important or that it is a fantasy. Imagination is our most important human feature. When used in a positive way, it will lead us to greatness. Through our imagination, we feed the soul and then in return the soul feeds us creative impulses to follow.

Are bodies really so important if we end up discarding them one day? Our bodies are temples for the light of God, and, yes, they are very important. Our bodies express our present selves. Bodies are amazing because they can change and heal and surprise all of the scientific world's fixed beliefs by doing the unexpected. Our minds are our bodies. There is no separation. There are conversations that take place all over our bodies that originate from a main source–our minds. The communication can get a bit confused when we are damaged or we have allowed separation from our God-self. Regardless of their age, shape, or condition, our bodies are exciting instruments of God.

Our minds are our spirits. So if we keep our minds free from debris, our spirits are then free, too. One way to keep our minds fresh and happy is to express our whole selves–body, mind, spirit, and soul. Find a positive way to express your whole self, and you will lead a full and rewarding, spiritual life.

Self-Expression

1. How do you use your body to express yourself? How could the angels help you take it further? Think of your imagination, soul, and spirit and ask the same questions.

2. Think about how you express yourself by your choice of music, colors, styles, books, and friends and by knowing the angels. Do the following:

- List ways you are currently expressing yourself.
- List ways you expressed yourself as a child.
- List ways you expressed yourself as a young adult or teenager.
- List ways you would like to express yourself.
- List things you are good at but don't always do.

3. Think about your life at the present, and list situations, events, and things that you believe would make your life easier and more creative. For example, "When I move, I would have more time to create," or "When I get more money . . . " Then list things that make your life run smoothly now.

4. List some ways you could make more time to be creative. Maybe you spend more time than you need to talking on the phone, watching television, and so on. Think about how you spend your days, and you will probably find some extra

time to add more creativity. Keep adding to this list. When you discover a pattern, make a note of it.

5. I talked about body, spirit, and soul above and using mind as spirit. Quite often, body, mind, and spirit are represented as a triangle. Think of your own triangle, or trinity—a group of three—however you like. The holy trinity is the parent, child, and Holy Spirit. The trinity makes one Godhead. Think of trinities in your own life that make up the one you. Play with a triangle and add things to it. Invite the angels in for inspiration.

6. How can the angels help you express your true self?

Moods and Emotions

When our feelings are violent or wrathful, we can transform them into powerful art rather than venting them on the world. Such art helps us accept that aspect of ourselves. Self-acceptance is paramount to compassion for others.

Natalie Rogers, *The Creative Connection: Expressive Arts as Healing*

A mood is a temporary state of mind or of spirits. The word *mood* is also used to describe the feeling or tone conveyed by a literary or artistic work. Moods don't have to be taken seriously, but they can be very good fuel for creativity. If you find you are in a good mood, you will most likely want to express joy. If you find yourself in a "bad" mood, there is no reason not to express it in an artistic fashion. Maybe you are feeling down and out. Maybe you're experiencing anger, grief, sadness, or another state that isn't particularly pleasant. Use the energy of an angry or a sorrowful moment in a creative encounter. Don't try and analyze your sorrow or feel guilty for feeling angry. Just find the energy and create something. Get out your journal and write. Write a story about someone who was very sad or angry, or simply write about your feelings—all of them.

When I was studying acting, I had a difficult time understanding what emotions were. I was always afraid I didn't really *have* emotions. How could I expect to be an actress if I didn't have emotions? Now I realize it would be impossible to be human without them. And although emotions can be uncomfortable at times, they are always present waiting to be expressed or dealt with. Emotion is feeling; it is an energy that moves through us. The presence of fear and anger can sometimes stop our emotional energy from running its course. Creative expression can help unblock the path by allowing us to deal with the fear and anger constructively. It offers a perfect way for us to *grow* through our fear or anger instead of just *going* through a painful or depressing time.

You can have a lot of fun being dramatic with your moods and emotions. Don't make excuses for your moods. Make art. This can be done very simply with some crayons, or you can get yourself some paints and a canvas. It may help to put on some music to go with your mood. Although most of the ideas I suggest in this book have to do with lighter qualities, qualities that the angels encourage, I think it would be both ridiculous and boring to imagine that we are going to feel up, blissful, and happy all the time. Basically, the angels are able to help you best when you are truly and honestly being yourself. The angels are our spiritual helpers, and they are ready to help us through the dark times. The negative effects that come from a negative state happen because we don't express our negativity in a constructive way. As long as our moods don't cause the world to suffer, we can use them in our creativity, while we wait for the day to come when we are totally enlightened and never in a bad mood (ha ha!).

Expressing Yourself in the Moment

1. Don't wait for outside inspiration. Use whatever you're experiencing in the moment and express it—regardless of the tone. Our creative self is always ready to express life, and life is always a surprise with the angels nearby.

2. Get out your journal, and write about your emotions. Use the stream-of-consciousness technique, and keep emotion and mood in your mind as you follow the streams. Think about the freedom children have in expressing their emotions. When you are doing your stream-of-consciousness writing, let yourself laugh, cry, scream, or sing out loud. Get used to simple and basic expression.

3. Grab your sketchbook and some crayons or charcoal, and express your mood and emotions. Be wild and brave with your drawing or expression. Use symbols and colors to express how you feel.

4. The angels don't leave you or sit in judgment when you are in a bad mood. They won't encourage your bad mood, but they won't punish you by leaving, because they know moods are temporary. What the angels will do is shine their love light a little stronger in your direction. If you find yourself in a mood

you want to change, all you have to do is take a moment and become aware of this light. The light will bring awareness and love, and awareness and love give you the choice to be who you are with trust. Be true to yourself at all times. If you have a mood to deal with, don't deny its presence. Be creative and you will have fun with your moods and be able to take life much more lightly.

Expressing an Attitude

An attitude is a way of thinking or behaving. We can choose our attitudes, and sometimes it is fun to create an attitude and stick with it if we need to change our perception on something.

Choosing Your Attitude

1. If you are upset over something that has happened to you and it makes you sad and angry, choose to create an attitude of rejoicing, because whatever is making you upset is a lesson that will free you in some way. Play the game "This is the happiest day of my life" by repeating this phrase, telling the angels, and then finding a reason for it to be so. You will find yourself happier each day you play.

2. Think of an attitude and meditate on it. Think of what goes with it–what behaviors and thinking patterns result. Think of how attitudes help you express yourself. Think of what attitudes the angels carry.

3. Here are some possible attitudes to ponder: happy, open, peaceful, graceful, loving, grateful, whimsical, mirthful, light, and so forth.

Gestalt Therapy and Self-Expression

I was introduced to Gestalt therapy at a young age, and the rules and philosophy have stayed with me ever since. One thing I like about the philosophy is that it helps us become authentic and true to the moment, which helps us get closer to the angels. I thought I would share a few of the principles of Gestalt with you, in case you are not familiar with them, to help you expand your self-expression. These principles, or "rules of the game," of course only apply where appropriate in the context. *Gestalt* means whole, and the psychology is the study of a person as a *whole* responsible for his or her own being.

One rule (game technique) or idea concerns "it" language and "I" language. This particular rule helps us with responsibility and owning our bodies and behaviors. For example, we often refer to our bodies in the third person—"it" language. If you have a pain, you might say, "It hurts," so you would change that to "I hurt." Or if you referred to your hand as "it," a Gestalt therapist would ask you to use "I" and refer to what your hand is doing. Sometimes we make statements such as "It is raining" or "It feels weird in here" to describe what is happening around us. Again, you would put "I" in place of "it" and realize that you are the one feeling weird or rainy. So this is one game a therapist plays.

Other games include changing "can't" to "won't." Again, the aim is to put the responsibility on us. Often we say, "Oh, I just *can't* do that," thinking we don't have the capability or power, when what we really mean is we *won't* do it. Of course, there are some things we can't do, so this only applies if we are using *can't* as an excuse. Other points to think about include: "Trying" means "not doing" or "won't do." "Should" and "ought" equal "will" or "won't." "But" eliminates what you just said. For example, in the sentence "I like him, but I think he is a bad person," *but* in this sentence separates what is said, so a therapist would ask you to change "but" to "and" for more clarity. Other ideas include:

- Guilt is unexpressed resentment.
- Sometimes questions can be a lazy way out.
- Turning questions into statements to define what is really being requested is also a game to play.

Sometimes it is fun to go over things you have written in your journals and use these rules and discover other meanings and truths.

The "awareness continuum" is an important Gestalt tool used to find out what you are experiencing in the moment. The therapist continually brings you back to the present by asking you what you are aware of right now. This helps you get away from explaining experiences and interpreting behavior and get on the road to simply being aware in the moment and relying on the senses. Being fully aware in the moment—of body feelings, sensations, and perceptions—is really the only thing we know for certain.

Living in the now is a central theme of Gestalt therapy. The following ideas are found in various Gestalt therapy writings concerning living in the now. I summarize them here.

- Live now. Be concerned with the present rather than with the past or future.
- Live here. Deal with what is present rather than what is absent. Deal with the moment at hand.

- Stop imagining. Experience the real—this very physical moment.
- Stop unnecessary thinking. Rather, taste and see.
- Express rather than manipulate, explain, justify, or judge.
- Give in to unpleasantness and pain just as to pleasure. Do not restrict your awareness.
- Accept no "should" or "ought" other than your own; cease using "shoulds" with other people.
- Take full responsibility for your actions, feelings, and thoughts.
- Surrender to being as you are.

I added this brief Gestalt therapy information to help you express and communicate in the clearest and most authentic way. If you are interested in more information regarding Gestalt psychology, check your local library or bookstore for some of the many titles available.

Mandalas

The contemplation of a mandala is meant to bring an inner peace, a feeling that life has again found its meaning and order.
Marie Louise von Franz, Man and His Symbols

Mandala is a Hindu word meaning magic circle. Jung used mandalas as an expression of the human psyche and saw constructing them as a way to restore inner balance and understanding. Mandalas are also used by some cultures as a meditation tool to enable the person to achieve deep meditation.

Making a Mandala

1. Making mandalas is a fun way to express yourself. The basic rules are simple. First you make a circle. A compass or plate can help you achieve this. Next you designate four main points within the circle, which represent the four directions, or the four seasons/archangels, or the four elements—earth, fire, water, air. You can have more than four points, but for starters four is a good way to create mandalas. The center—the focal

point—represents you, so the next step is to choose an image or symbol that will represent you at this moment. You can also choose four images for the four points, each representing an aspect of yourself. At this point, draw the images or find pictures and make a collage of them in the circle in the appropriate areas.

2. You can make a mandala for almost anything you want insight on—special self-healing, relationship issues, angel consciousness, nature, and career mandalas. After they are finished, keep them in sight for a week or so to remind you of the symbols and images that help you in your life.

3. It is very important for an artist to have inner peace. Many artists I know are very peaceful, and others seem to only have their peace when they are painting or creating. Mental peace is like water for your creative growth. Create your own special mandala of peaceful creative energy to play with and to use as a visual point of concentration for meditating on the angelic realm and absorbing the creative peace always available to you.

Symbolic Play

Becoming aware of special symbols or images in your everyday life that mean something important to you, or that help you express a part of yourself, provides fun and is a good way to express yourself. Start thinking about them, and what they mean to you, and use them actively in your life. These symbols or images may appear in synchronisms or in special messages. You can use them to give you hope when they appear in your world. Think of your special symbols as an extension of your present self. Make a mandala of them.

Here are some of my favorite symbols and images, with a "flash thought" about what they mean to me:

- Birds: The angels' special pets.
- Sun: The golden life force of creation, regeneration, growth.
- Moon: The silver light of peace; the angels reflecting glass to watch over and bless the world.
- Rainbows and sun birds: Watercolors from the angels.
- Clouds: Heavenly clay for the angels.
- Trees: Masterpieces from the angels.
- Flowers: Art projects from the angels; special mandalas to remind you of divine bliss.

Your Symbols

1. Make a list of your symbols, and put a "flash thought" after each one.

2. A medicine bag is a little pouch you wear around your neck. Inside the pouch you can carry symbolic items that have personal and generally recognizable significance. Create an angel medicine bag, with rocks, gems, religious medals, flowers, and whatever else you associate with the angelic realm.

3. Build your own creativity angel shrine. Collect items that are symbolic to you and that you feel help strengthen your creative spirit. Place them on your shrine with other important items. Make sure one represents your direct connection to the divine, for example, an angel statue.

4. Remember the song from *The Sound of Music* called "My Favorite Things"? Make a list of *your* favorite things. Make a mandala, painting, or a collage of your favorite things and keep it near you.

5. Do an oracle mandala, using five points, representing a five-point star. Let the top of the star represent your head—divine connection. You can designate the other points to represent whatever you feel fits. Then pull cards or some other type of oracle tool for each point and write them in around the circle. Then draw in the images and symbols that are related in your mind.

6. Have a "self-expression party" where people come expressing themselves symbolically, however they choose. You can go around in a circle and have each person share his or her images and symbols, and why they are important.

Color

There are colors for every angel. Color is something we see only in certain dimensions, but hues exist on the spiritual plane much finer than the colors we experience. When we let color speak to us in its true celestial language, we begin to communicate with angelic beings.
K. Martin-Kuri

As white light passes through a prism, it breaks down into all of its component parts—the spectrum of color. Levanah Shell Bdolak states that, "Color is the phenomenon of light. It is the wave length vibration of light moving. And we, as Spiritual Beings, are bodies of light. Our energy and our energy centers (chakras) are fine-tuned machines created in a body of light." Color is a way we express ourselves. Sometimes when we create something, colors become a message from the unconscious mind. Here are some possible meanings for a few colors. You may have a different experience of these colors, so keep notes about what each color means to you in your journal.

- Pink: Love.
- Red: Primary; warm; gives back light; fire, blood, birth, war, passion, raw energy, intense.
- Orange: Combines red and yellow; warm, energy, activity, fire, butterfly, pumpkin, enduring energy.
- Yellow: Primary; intellect, faith, manifestation, mind, mental energy, joy.
- Green: Combines yellow and blue; gives back light and absorbs it; nature, spirit healing, nurture, freedom from the past, calming, learning, "Go."
- Blue: Primary; cool; absorbs the light; sensitivity, truth, loyalty, peace, clarity; sky blue is the color of Mary, Queen of the Angels.
- Indigo: Deep connection with spirit; free spirit, rare, abstract, absolute.
- Purple: Spiritual integrity, inner royalty, justice, fortune, noble, majestic.
- Gold: Sun; God as light; glory, radiance.
- Silver: Moon, reflection; reduces inner fear.
- White: The highest vibration; the combination of all the colors at once; purity, transcendence, innocence, sacred, positive thinking.
- Iridescent: Otherworldly, altered states, imagination, dreams, ethereal.
- Black: Authority, clergy, mystery, darkness; the absence of color.
- Brown: Earth.

Angels hold converse with each other and with mortals by means of color. An assemblage of angels when engaged in healing prayers for the bestowal of blessings upon humanity appear as a glory of variegated clouds that fleck the sky in the hours of dawn or at sunset time.
Corinne Heline

Natural Essence

There is a part of each of us that is of the same essence as the devas. We might call that the soul level, or the spirit. Thus any of us can "listen to" and "talk" with the angelic world, because we share the same worlds within us. Love and appreciation are the bridges between us.
Dorothy Maclean, *To Honor the Earth*

We live on a planet called earth. The God Spirit of the planet is nature, or, if you prefer, Mother Nature. Being heavenly does not mean we deny our connection to earth. Being close and physical with nature is a step toward understanding God. Nature offers a physical connection to the divine. It is interesting to me that a lot of "worldly and societal" problems originate from the top floors of office buildings, far away from trees and birds, far away from the soil and rocks of the earth, with filtered air and no views but other buildings–how unnatural.

Humans sometimes separate themselves from nature with the thought pattern "We are here and nature is out there; God is up there and we are down here." There is no separation, and if we truly realize this, we will make choices that are in accordance with God, heaven, and nature. If we love the feel of the sun on our face, if we jump for joy at a beautiful sunset, if we celebrate the natural world, this does not mean we have become heathens. God is everywhere. We stand on holy ground.

Getting "back to nature" is a great way to expand our creativity. In my mind, there is nothing better than a nice, peaceful walk outside. It really doesn't matter where you take your walk, as long as natural vegetation is around. Stop and notice anything that interests you in the natural world. An unusual shape or a flower you have never seen may catch your eye; stop and study it. Ask the angels for insight. I think one of the best ways to learn to draw is to go outside and draw trees, branches, leaves, and so forth. Staying close to nature will give you a healthy body, mind, spirit, and soul.

Angels of the land – nature spirits – watch over the growth of plants and trees. You can connect with these spirits by listening and tuning into the creative energy of the landscape around you. Just as all the natural colors of the landscape never clash, the more natural we become and live, the less we clash with nature. Our goal is to live in harmony with the forces of nature.

Back to Nature

1. One way to get in tune with the beauty of nature is to take a sketchbook and a pen or pencil with you when you are out near the trees and flowers and sky and sketch what you see. Even if you don't feel that you can easily sketch nature, do it anyway. Do it not with the idea in mind of creating a perfect drawing, but so that you will begin to see what you are looking at. This process is about discovery, and art is discovery. Look closely at the bark of a tree, then sketch it. Stand back and

look at the whole tree, then sketch it. Look at the dirt, then sketch it. Try sketching without looking at your paper. Experiment and play. Close your eyes and sketch. Free your hand, free your nature, and have fun.

2. Have a picnic in your favorite park, and invite the angels and nature spirits. Interview them about their environment. Get your journal and write down any messages. Go on a hike in the woods, walk on the beach, get in touch with the desert, and look for new avenues of nature to explore and listen to. Read *To Hear the Angels Sing* by Dorothy Maclean for inspiration (see the Book and Resource List).

3. Find a stream, fountain, waterfall, pond, or pool—any place where sunlight shines on water. Watch the reflected light in the water and absorb the psychic energy reflected by the light. Ask the angels to raise your vibration and bring you joy. As you watch the sunlight dance on the water, review your recent activities and look for patterns and awarenesses.

4. Sit quietly in a park, a garden, or your yard. Close your eyes, and focus on the energy of growth and regeneration that is happening all around you. Connect with this energy until you can actually hear, feel, see, and smell the growth vibrations. Use this energy in your own life. Ask the angels to help regenerate all the healthy cells in your body. Visualize all your organs with renewed life and vigor.

5. Go to a nursery and pick out a plant by feeling only. Don't base your choice on how it looks but on how it makes you feel. Let the angels guide you. Then study your plant's essence. Look for information about the plant, and get to know its vibrational level. Use it as a meditation or prayer partner.

6. Plant a small garden and designate it a mind garden.

You don't need to plant a large one; even a window box will do. Pick out some seeds to plant. As you plant them, think of how the soil is like your mind, and the seeds are like thoughts and ideas. Pay close attention to the stages of growth, and use these stages to represent areas of your life. Play with the idea. Get in touch with how growth really takes place, and explore the symbolism of life.

7. Look for other ways that growth in nature represents us. Plant a vine and study the symbolism. Plant vegetables and enjoy a harvest of abundance. Plant flowers to soothe and bless your soul. Live near trees for strength and the protection of their shade. Think of the connection to the sun, air, and water—all necessary for growth and fruition.

8. Think of how we use the term *grounded* and reflect on how vitally important grounding is to plants. If you need grounding, imagine your invisible roots going into the ground for nourishment and stability. Eating potatoes and rice is a good grounding tool. Use your imagination to discover the nature spirits and their guardianship over the plants and animals. Compare this relationship to the one you have with your own guardian angel. These are the seed thoughts; let them germinate in your own imagination. You will have fun if you do.

9. Study flowers and keep a little section about your favorite flowers in your journal. Study aromatherapy and consult herb books. Read about Bach flower remedies (see the Book and Resource List). The more in tune you are with the angels, the more you will understand how important flowers and herbs are to you. Flowers are heavenly creations that the angels are directly responsible for. I like to think of flowers as the art projects of the angels. Life outdoors is the angels' art gallery.

Flowers have a direct effect on our souls. When you read about Bach flower remedies, you will understand how amazing flowers are. Grow your favorite flowers and herbs. Learn how to make tea and potpourri, and pursue other fun and creative projects with herbs and flowers.

Miscellaneous Ideas

Recycling

1. Recycle with art and creativity in mind. When you find something—a block of wood, a good piece of cardboard, or a card—hold it for a moment and ask your inner muse for ideas about how to create art with it. Or just save things. When the ideas surface, you will have stuff ready to play with.

Brush Strokes

1. Start a small collection of watercolor brushes in different sizes and shapes. Whenever you feel like it, get some watercolors (inexpensive ones will do) and play with brush strokes. You can also use ink in an interesting way. Don't try to create anything in particular. Just play with the various ways to use a paint brush. Then play with color combinations and have fun.

Creating With a Child

1. If you have children or work with children, don't be afraid to finger paint or make mud castles with them. Write silly

stories. Get some poster paint and paint a tree, a house, and a sun. If you don't have children around, maybe you can volunteer to help out at a nearby school.

Closing Thoughts to Chapter 4

The Sacredness of the Creative Project

When something is sacred, it is to be regarded with the utmost respect and reverence. A creative project is sacred and needs to be treated as such—not exploited or misused. Someone wise once told me that when you begin a project, you can think of it first as an embryo. Treat it as you would an embryo. Even a pinprick could destroy an embryo. Think of a pinprick as a negative thought from someone discouraging you at this stage. Therefore, don't tell many people (maybe no one) about your project when it is in the embryo stage. The next stage could be thought of as a fetus. At this point, your project is still in a fragile space, but a pinprick won't kill it. It still has to develop, so care is needed in nurturing and preparing a proper environment for growth. Next comes birth, and your creative project becomes a baby and requires all the attention you would give a baby. You feel protective and constantly alert to its needs. When your project becomes a child, you begin to allow it out into the world alone, but with a watchful and careful eye. Of course, don't take this idea too seriously. It is just a metaphor to play with that has been helpful to me in the past. Another way to use this metaphor is to think of the seed, sprout, sapling, and finally tree.

What to Do With a Finished Creative Project

Creativity doesn't always mean you end up with an actual product or project, but when you do it helps to think about what is most important—the process or the product. Not all creative projects need to be commercially bound. Many times in my life I have chosen an art form to explore simply for the therapeutic benefits, and I have truly enjoyed what I have created. Sometimes no one else sees my creations and drawings until years later or not at all. You don't have to be a famous singer to enjoy singing. You don't have to have a gallery showing to enjoy painting. Too often people start a creative project with the intention of showing it to the world right away, gearing their actions to please the world or to fit into a current interest. This is not a recommended way to tap into the realm of spiritual creativity. Sometimes this might seem to be a way to make a lot of money—following the fads and so forth—but money comes and goes and so do fads. Do what your heart guides you to do, and you may end up creating a new and original interest wave. Don't jump on the bandwagon. Go your own way.

The Ebb and Flow of the Creative Drive

There is a natural energy pattern to the creative drive—action, cultivation, then quiet incubation time. If there is all action, there will be very little integration of inspiration and little time to truly connect with the angels and the natural world. Make sure you integrate balance into your creativity. On days when you are not inspired to act out your creative drive, take a break and know that taking this rest may be the most crucial thing you can do for your creative flow. Don't judge a quiet day as non-creative or uninspired. Just take some time off–be bored even–but trust that there is more going on than is readily present to your physical senses and moods. No matter what you are creating, whether it is a solution to a problem or a project, you must allow time for incubation. *Incubation* means "to cause to develop under suitable situations."

Pay attention to thoughts that come when you are relaxed or doing something that frees your mind. Oftentimes, I get thoughts when I am in the shower. I call them my "shower thoughts." As soon as I finish my shower, I write them down, and they have been very helpful for developing ideas. If you ever get stuck or bothered by something in the midst of a creative encounter, stop what you are doing and go lie down and breathe deeply. Clear your mind with each breath. This can give you quick insight, new inspiration, new ideas, and a fresh approach to take when you go back to what you were doing.

Remember that truth is a pathless land, and sometimes our creativity is fostered when we are wandering aimlessly. Don't be afraid to be aimless and without direction. Don't let goal-directed belief systems keep you from discovering who you are and what you want to create. Daydream, let your mind wander, let go of strict goals–in other words, take a vacation from the pressures of being someone and you will find out who you really are.

Part Three
Angel-Guided Journeys

About Part Three

This section consists of three angel-guided journeys, designed either to read or to use as guided meditations. I chose this format to speak from heart to heart—hoping to release much of the intellectual reasoning and logic we batter ourselves with all day long. With these meditations, I hope to help you get used to the idea of going within for spiritual nourishment and strength.

Once you read through one of these journeys and truly let it touch you, you will never be the same. You will begin to expand and change as you accept the many parts of yourself with love. Self-love will nurture and nourish you. Once you are aware of the love you have for yourself, it will expand to all areas of your life. The journey is a process set in motion by your acceptance of love, the law of grace, and your request for divine help.

Ready yourself for the journeys in whatever way makes you feel most comfortable. You may find you are ready after a few relaxing deep breaths, or you may want to repeat a mantra or prayer first. Most importantly, create a sacred and safe space for yourself. You can do this by simply declaring that you are safe and protected and ready to journey with your guardian angel to meet your new angel guide. Define your sacred space with candle light, music, flowers, special stones, and a special crystal to hold. Burn incense or an aromatherapy lamp containing your favorite oil. Have fun with the idea of creating sacred space. The main idea is to take it lightly—not seriously. In this way, you engage your unconscious mind, where seeds of self-love are anxious to germinate.

The journeys may come alive in your dreamtime, meaning you may journey further in your sleep. So ask your angel guide to come to you in a dream to guide you and expand the teachings while you are asleep. Words are powers unto themselves, so reading the journeys with this in mind will have an effect on you. There is nothing negative about or in the journeys. The angels have only love for you. Angel journey experiences allow you to grow and know yourself and your soul's mission, so in turn you will find it easier to love yourself and your life.

If you want to encourage a meditative state for the journey, center yourself by taking deep, slow breaths that fill your being with light. Feel the light traveling through your body and connecting you to the earth for grounding. Your guardian angel is always at your side or right behind you. Your guardian angel's wings hold love energy close to you. Feel the warmth this brings to your being.

If you alter your waking state for the journey, it is important after the journey to come back to your physical reality. Breathe yourself awake by imagining each breath of air containing energizing, clean oxygen. This will help reground you. The herb rosemary is a good scent for clearing the mind. Anytime you need help, ask your guardian angel or repeat the affirmation to the Archangel St. Michael three times: "Divine Light of the highest order under the protection of the Archangel Saint Michael."

Angel Guides

You will meet angel guides on the journeys who you may not have known were there for you. These guides are available if you want to make up your own self-love and soul evolvement council, for the advancement and expansion of your purpose for being here on earth. This council will be on hand, at all times, to guide you in decisions and creative choices and will always be sending you messages of love. Your guides will help you align your soul with your personality, through refinement and by acquiring virtuous qualities. And your guides will help you take your innate creativity to heavenly heights.

The angel guides are guardians of a particular universal energy system to tap into. Positive energy systems in the universe are guarded by the angels. When you allow a particular energy system to flow through your system in a harmonious way, a magnetic field is created that attracts positive energy to you, which in turn allows you to transcend human limitations your mind may have set up. By connecting with certain energy systems, you can blast through negative programs that cause you to repeat negative habits. You may notice changes immediately, or change may be a slower process. Just remember that by engaging the angels in a process of change, it is always for your highest *spiritual* (not worldly) good.

Recording Your Experience

After each journey, you can ask yourself questions, such as:

- What did your guide look like?
- What is your guide's name?
- What feelings did you have on the journey?
- What colors did you see around your angel guide? (You may find one color stands out, and that color acts as the

ray on which your angel guide will connect with you and your guardian angel.)

- Any new thoughts about love?
- What human blocks will you now transcend by releasing to the angels?
- Did you sense a name for your guide or guardian angel?
- Did any scent come to you?
- What energy systems did you learn to tap into?

Chapter 5
Self-Love and Acceptance

If you allow it, this journey will help you get past reasons and excuses and forge ahead into the everlasting wonderful effects of true self-love.

Close your eyes. Relax your physical being. Breathe deeply. Each breath brings the angels closer to you. Your cares are drifting away. The "noise" of the world is silenced. You are in a sacred space protected by the heavenly Creator and the angels. Each breath opens your heart. Through your heart, your mind softens and absorbs the beauty and love of the realm of heaven. Feel your breath enter through your heart and expand up through your mind and out into the universal energy system of love. As you leave the world behind you, comfortably align yourself with, and become one with, your guardian angel.

You now find yourself waiting in a dense midnight blue fog with your guardian angel by your side. You see nothing, but feel a loving presence coming your way. An angel teacher comes to guide you on a journey of self-love and acceptance. Take a moment to become familiar with your guide through feeling. Get a sense of his or her presence, yet you cannot see your guide because you are engulfed in the dense blue fog.

As you wait before the gateway to the energy system of pure love light, your guide asks: "*Are you willing to love and accept yourself now, to transcend the trivial human setbacks that make you feel unworthy of love?*" If you answer yes, you are ready to journey through this gateway with your special teacher.

All you can see is the deep blue fog, but you feel safe and protected as your guide gently takes your hand. Your guide sends you a loving thought about how special you are, and this makes you feel innocent as a child. Something else happens as this loving feeling takes hold in your consciousness. The fog begins to lift, and little flecks of light float around you like stars in the heaven. Feel and delight in the little flecks of colorful light. Each one is a thought of how special you are. Now it is your turn to send yourself a loving thought. Keep in mind that you are in a sacred space where the thoughts of others will not reach you. You are at one with your angels and God. Think of something wonderful about yourself—not what someone else thinks, something *you* like about yourself. If you start to feel silly or you find that you are doing too much thinking, then take a moment to relax and re-center. Simply allow feelings of love for yourself to emerge. Here they come. Now bask in the light of self-love.

More of the fog lifts and stars disappear, and you notice a golden light growing bright like the sun rising in the east. Now the mist has taken on a sparkling pink hue. Your guide takes you a step forward. You hear the voice within, the voice that encourages you to love yourself. You will hear this voice often from now on. Your angel guide asks you to keep generating loving thoughts and feelings about yourself, one after the other as quickly as you can. With each loving thought, more of the fog disappears. Eventually, you find yourself fully in the golden light as you step forward on the path of self-love with your angelic guide from the energy system of divine love. You have a good idea of who your angel guide is and what he/she looks like. You may only see light, you may only feel a presence, or you may see an angel with wings. The appearance of your angel guide is up to your special and private imagination. Cultivate a sense of the love that exists in this realm you have entered. You will want to tap into this realm in the future. Your sense of it now will allow you to feel it and access it again when you need to.

Looking ahead, you see a beautiful archway made of a gridwork of pink light. You discover that you can control the radiance of everything around you by the levels of love you generate for yourself. The more blasts of love you give yourself, the brighter this special world becomes, and you start to gain your heaven vision. With heaven vision, everything looks iridescent. Light is splashed with spectrums of colors you have never seen before. You notice something else has happened. Your body has become so light you hardly notice it. In fact, you seem to be gliding in synch with your angel guide as you float through the gateway of pink light.

Once inside the gate, your guide begins to teach. You notice some large rocks perfect for sitting on, perfect for having a conversation. As you sit down on your rock, a grotto appears. Water is gently trickling and bouncing off the rocks and ferns that make up this grotto, and light catches the drops, sending off rays of heavenly colors. The beauty of this grotto is intoxicating, and you feel giddy and light with joy. You are attracted to something glowing in the center of the grotto. It looks like a key, and your teacher sends you the thought that in time you will know that what is glowing is a gift for you.

Now it is time to explore some self-love ideas. Your teacher speaks. *"Idea exploration number one is: Accept yourself exactly as you are at this moment in time. You are who you are right now for a specific reason and regardless of what you think is good or bad, right or wrong, with your life, you must accept life as perfect in being just what it is. You are perfect in being who you are right now. You have the choice to accept all parts of yourself."*

The teacher pauses. You ask questions, but your teacher is quiet, because the answers are within you. You must now internalize what is told to you before your teacher will go further. A light flashes. It happens. You accept it all—you surrender your ideas of who you should be and how life should be. Now trees appear around the grotto, bringing you strength. You know that whenever you see a tree from now on, it will give you strength to accept yourself and your life.

Your teacher smiles and sends a blessing to your soul. Your teacher speaks again. *"Idea two is that human life is basically good. Your life is good; it is special. You are in this world but not of the worldly illusion that goes on outside your door. You belong to heaven. Love your frailty and your humanity. It connects you to the creative force in the universe and allows you to love other humans and their frailty. As you love the weakness of being human, you will grow strong inside. You will know the power of unconditional love—the one power that will make you whole."* This idea leaves you a bit confused. Frailty and weakness don't exactly seem to be admirable traits. You ask your teacher about this, and again there is silence. Then you realize there are some things about being human that can get out of control in your life. When you try to control something and push the river in the wrong direction, you become weak and exhausted. Turning to the Higher Power of unconditional love (God) and giving over your control, you become strong. You learn ways of being that give you strength. You know life is good and you will change what you can and leave the rest to God. With this realization, your teacher points to a large rainbow stretching over the grotto and the trees. The rainbow represents hope. From now on, whenever you see a rainbow in the sky or reflected through prisms, you will gain a surge of hope for all of humanity and nature.

Your teacher laughs, and you feel the laughter resonate in your soul. You begin to laugh, too, because life is so humorous. Life is good. You feel good and happy. It is time for the third self-love exploration. You look at your teacher, and you see a mirror with your own reflection. Your teacher speaks. *"Talk to the person you see in this mirror and tell him/her you will no longer reject him/her. Starting now, you are willing to love the person in the mirror. You know you are willing. Self-love begins with willingness. Look at your smile. You do love yourself, and this is okay. You are beautiful. Be kind to yourself. Reach out to your reflection, and hug yourself. You are life divine—you are love itself. You will know the power of love like never before, for you are willing to really love life itself—yourself."*

The mirror is gone, and your teacher is silent. You are wondering if you really do love yourself. Then you realize that thought itself knows nothing of love. Love is a power, and you are willing to feel it. At this realization, the area around the grotto comes alive with flowers, birds, and animals. Life is dancing all around you. You see the nature spirits dwelling in the trees of strength. You feel the rainbow of hope vibrating with love.

Your angel guide takes the glowing object you were attracted to and hands it to you. It is a gift to remind you that you are loved in heaven, and the more you generate this heavenly love for yourself the more magnificent life will be. You hold the key, the gift in your hand, and look at how beautiful it is. Suddenly the flowing gift implants itself in your heart. You will never be the same. You are transformed by self-love. You thank your angel guide and then thank yourself. You suddenly get the urge to yell out something like "I love, therefore I am!" A blast of divine self-love comes your way, and you realize the journey has only just begun.

You have returned with the key to self-love. Make your key real in your life. Find a material object, such as a favorite stone or an old key, and keep it with you to remind you of self-love.

Chapter 6
Back to the Source

An angel is a being of light from the realm of heaven. Many people believe that they came directly from the heaven realm into the earth realm. Others feel they have come from other realms or from other star systems. For the sake of this journey, explore the idea that you came here directly from the heaven realm. Right before you entered the physical plane, you were at one with the angels, playing and generating joy and love. In heaven, all light beings guard the sacred qualities of love, joy, happiness, mirth, peace, and divine humor. These qualities are kept alive by the exchange going on between humans and angels. Humans need help keeping sacred qualities alive on the earth, and this is why we have a guardian angel. Our guardian angel protects our spirituality by reminding us of who we really are. Our guardian is our angelic reflection. For this journey, you will return to heaven for a view of your angelic reflection. You may want to declare that you will be an angel-in-training here in the earth realm. This means you will vow to keep alive the qualities of heaven here on earth. When you declare yourself an angel-in-training, you will find that you naturally vibrate to a higher frequency, that you will be able to tune into the realm of heaven in your meditations and spiritual practices.

Your guardian angel has known you since the beginning of your soul's first imprint. You will now merge in complete alignment with your guardian angel. You feel comfortable and at peace. With each breath, your heart opens, and love flows in from the divine source of all life. Warm, glowing peace surrounds you and washes through your mind, cleansing the window of your soul. Your feelings of well-being are expanding, and you begin to feel your entire body tuning to light. You are now in tune with the light vibrations of the heaven realm. You are in complete alignment with your higher self/guardian angel.

You are feeling a bit sleepy, and this reminds you of the sleepy feelings you had as a baby. A cloud of pink light appears, and you lie down to rest your body. You are now floating upward on your cloud. You are not afraid because you know you are at one with your guardian angel. The dense physical world has disappeared, and you find yourself in a world of bright colors, dancing stars, and lively spirit forms. You recognize the sounds, the sights, and the sweet scents. You hear a soft singing off in the distance. The sounds are sweet and clear. You're hearing a song of love–a choir of angels singing praises to the heavenly Creator, the divine life force–the highest vibration of love in the universe.

You find yourself gliding toward a light you recognize as your favorite color. As you get closer to this light, you see that it is a doorway and that a baby angel–a cherub–is waiting for you. The baby angel will be your guide through the doorway of your special color. Your guide is a baby, and yet you receive a sense of true wisdom along with pure innocence. Take a moment to communicate with your guide. A name may come to you. Your guide asks if you are ready to journey through the doorway leading to the realm of heaven. Are you ready to view your own angelic reflection? You answer yes and find yourself in heaven.

All around you is the divine play of the universe. Angels are everywhere, and you witness streams of love radiating to earth. You are at the source. It is so beautiful that words are not necessary, thoughts have vanished, and you are at one with all that is love. Your guide takes you into the garden of reflections. Tall crystalline structures mirror the light and love energy that come their way. You now face one of the crystal structures, and the first thing you see is the most exquisite color you could imagine. This color is so beautiful it makes you giddy with mirth. You are viewing the special color of light that glows in your heart. It was created when you were. As you look directly into your heart-light, your angel guide asks you to view your angelic reflection. The experience is one of feelings as opposed to thoughts. What do you see in your mind's eye? How does your angelic reflection look to you? Take a good look and memorize yourself as the angel that you are. Ask questions of yourself. Find out more about who you really are. Ask your guide and guardian angel to allow you this vision of your angelic reflection to remain in your mind for whenever you may want to recall the vision. The pure wisdom and innocence of a child are yours. You have this within always. Now you will know how to tap the source when you need to lighten up for your earthly mission.

Now you are free to wander on this journey. If you generate the intent to view a certain aspect of your life through the eyes of an angel, it will happen in an instant. What is happening in your life that you would like a higher view of? What really matters to you? What brings true meaning to your life? Wander freely through these thoughts. Glide around through heaven, and enjoy all the wonders. You are at the source of all that reflects beauty and sweetness. What do you want to bring back to earth with you? Beauty soothes your soul on earth. Remember your visions of this heavenly beauty to tap into when needed.

Your baby angel reminds you it is time to return to the earth realm. Your guide tells you that you will view earth differently. Now that you have seen your own heavenly reflection, you will catch glimpses of angelic reflections in all the life on earth. Beauty will expand as you appreciate that it exists on earth–in nature, in people, in the starry sky, in art, and always in your heart. Your cloud appears, and that same sleepy feeling comes back to you.

You lie down on your cloud, and your baby angel tells you he/she will always be with you; whenever you need to view your inner angel child of wisdom, he/she will be with you. You arrive at the colored doorway, and your baby angel hands you a gift. Notice what it looks like. It will help you connect with your guide from the earth plane. You float away from the realm of heaven, through the doorway. Each slow breath you take expands throughout your body. You like your body. With each breath, your body becomes your friend. Your body is the home of your soul–your angelic reflection–and you are glad to be back on earth so you can fully enjoy the life that you are. Your guardian angel has taken a position in your higher self to light and guard you in all your ways on earth and beyond. One more deep breath of light, and you are back awake with an open heart. The journey has been accomplished.

You have returned with the knowledge of your angelic reflection. Make it real in your life.

Chapter 7

Venturing Into the Realms of Your Imagination

You and your guardian angel have an important date. You are scheduled to meet a muse from the realm of creative ideas to take you on a whirlwind tour of the senses. You have no time to think about what you may find, but a feeling of pure excitement is brewing inside you.

Your guardian angel has the map giving directions to where you will meet the muse. You have a thousand questions for your guardian angel as you find yourself walking along a beautiful mountain path. You ask: What is a muse? What does a muse look like? Are muses friendly? And so on. Your guardian angel informs you that although muses may seem harmless and full of good ideas, they can be a bit mischievous, like Puck. And that is why your guardian angel is going to stick close by you. As it happens, muses don't mean to cause trouble in people's lives; it is just that they don't have all the survival issues we have, such as eating, sleeping, drinking, and relating to other humans. So at times their inspiration can get intense and keep humans craving another realm and living only to create what they are experiencing in this other realm. Muses are attracted to humans who are using creative energy, and they want to help add a little fuel to the fire. Sometimes, too much fuel on a fire can be disastrous.

You feel you have been cautioned and well informed. Your guardian angel stops by a large rock, and you wait for the muse to come. You don't like the waiting. It seems that the muse is keeping you waiting too long, and your guardian angel gives you the message to look around at the beauty and not be so anxious. As you look around you, a sense of true beauty fills your soul. Just when you forget why you came, the muse jumps out of the large rock and lands in front of you, winking, with a sparkle in his or her eye. You know already that you have a character on your hands. You get the urge to giggle, but you don't want to upset anyone. Your guardian angel doesn't seem quite as impressed as you, but you notice a smile. You ask the muse if the rock is his or her home, and all you get is an "amusing" look in reply. Your guardian angel informs you that the muse won't talk in human language, but that you will get used to a different form of communication and you will understand.

The muse darts off on the mountain path, and you run along behind with an unfamiliar bounce in your step. A warm breeze is blowing, and it carries with it an intoxicating fragrance. You are feeling very giddy and light. The muse stops in front of a flowering vine that covers an entire hillside. One flower seems to be beckoning you closer and closer until you find you are standing inside the flower, with your guardian angel and the muse. The muse introduces you to the guardian spirit of the flower, and she looks just like the fairies in fairy tale books. She is able to talk to you, and you ask her where she gets the fragrance for her flower. She explains that the fragrance of a flower is a sweet thought from God that the guardian spirit attracts into the flower by its innate beauty. This makes perfect sense to you, and the muse jumps out of the flower. You and your guardian angel quickly follow.

The path is now following a stream, and you admire how the light reflects off the running water. The stream begins to make music. The notes are sweet, and the birds are joining in. Then a sound stops you with its beauty. An angelic choir is singing along, and everything around you is part of the harmony. A sound begins to come from inside you, not from your voice, but from your heart. It is a sweet note that harmonizes with the choir in its own unique way. You close your eyes and get closer to the note that your heart is singing. The notes are part of the great symphony of heaven, the cosmic dance, the song of the universe. The harmonic resonance is so pure that your being vibrates in bliss until you pass out completely and fall into the arms of your guardian angel.

You wake up in white space. Everything is clear, white space. The muse is hiding somewhere in this space, and you look everywhere trying to find him or her. Ladders of light suddenly appear, and you see the muse climbing one. Without thinking, you begin to climb a ladder, too. As you climb, you realize that the ladders are making up a giant gridwork of light rays, each a pure color ray with brilliant hues you have never imagined. As you look closer at a color ray, you notice that it has angels all through it. Then you follow the ray up and see that it comes from a point of light. The point of light is like an infinite diamond, reflecting all of these rays of colored light in different but certain directions. One light ray seems to be hitting the center of your soul. It is your favorite color, too. What luck that your favorite color light is reflecting into your heart center. A sudden realization surfaces: This light is your own part of the light of God, and it reflects from your soul outward. This realization sends you into a state of awe, at which time the muse pops out of nowhere and whisks you back to the mountain scene.

The muse is just staring at you, and you are getting a little nervous. At this point, your guardian angel tells you this means you have one travel request left, and the muse is waiting to know where to take you. Off in the distance, you notice a beautiful castle glowing like a sunset. This seems like a good place to visit, so you mention that and your muse laughs. He or she is quite happy to take you to that castle, and you are on your way. When you reach the threshold of the castle door, a sign appears above you and it reads, "You are entering the realm of creative ideas." This is better than you could have hoped for, and you step forward into the castle and find that your muse and guardian angel have stayed outside and are waving good-bye to you. You have stepped into a totally empty room. All you can see is completely empty space. Everything has been swept away. There is only nothingness—a big gap. You feel so disappointed. Not only are you alone, but this realm is like a vacuum—nothing to look at or experience. The other places you visited were so rich and alive, and now here you are in the middle of nothingness. You'd like to cry, but you are not sad. You try to laugh, but nothing happens. Then a spark of light appears in your mind. It opens the door into your imagination and you realize that you are the instrument, you are the cocreator. The source, the gap, is empty until a human makes contact with her or his own imagination and uses the energy through his or her own human system. Now you feel regenerated from the nothingness. It becomes raw energy waiting to be created. You would like to return back to the path, and the thought itself manifests you right back where you started, with your guardian angel close by. The muse's smiling face flashes before you, and this time *you* wink with a sparkle in *your* eye and wave good-bye, for now.

You have returned with blessings and privileges. Make them real in your life.

Part Four
Angel Forum on Creativity

About Part Four

We are all teachers for one another. Some of us may never be aware of our students, and others of us will. I asked some of my friends who are consciously living their creativity to share their points of view for this book. I wanted this to be a forum on creativity, intended to allow some discussion of the creative process that is unique in each one of us—because we are unique and original beings. I did not set up any rules for the people contributing. I just told them why I wanted them to contribute—so that others will be inspired to go forward with their own creative energy and so that what they had to say could reach others who are at the edge of a breakthrough.

The contributors to this section were not able to read this book before contributing, so I will say for the record that we all stand by our own feelings and opinions about creativity. Although there may be points where we differ, we all respect one another's experience. In other words, just because the contributors generously offered to be a part of this book does not mean they have to agree or be associated with everything I write. I am very grateful for and inspired by the contributions in this section, and I know you will be, too.

Chapter 8

It's a Creative Life!

Creativity

by K. Martin-Kuri

The subject of creativity is of immense importance to me not only from the viewpoint of my work as an angelologist but from that of an artist who paints images of heaven, an occasional poet who creates spiritual verse, and a teacher who seeks to explain the workings of the universe. I doubt if there is any part of my life not intimately involved with the daily process of creativity both on a personal and a professional level.

Creativity can best be understood if we remember the divine origins of the process. I believe there is only one first Creator who started all the many dimensions of existence—and the spiritual hierarchies, or angelic beings, are involved with the maintenance and development of that initial moment of divine thought that led to the creation of our universe. They are the active caretakers of the various heavens and the kingdoms of nature here on earth. And, of course, angels are involved with much more, especially the greatest creation of all, human life.

But there is another aspect to creativity that affects us and the world in which we live. We can either create from a sacred space in our inner consciousness or we can create from the lowest, most pained part of ourselves. When we create from that confused level, other than for the purposes of temporary therapeutic expression on a private basis, we become subject to the angels of destruction rather than the angels of love and light.

The question then arises: How can we create from a sacred space in which the angels of God can operate? I believe that to do this we need to arrive at a place of inner peace that establishes a stillness where the angels can offer the divine imaginations, inspirations, and intuitions that we seek.

To arrive at that inner calm does not mean ceasing activity. It means beginning to operate from a higher level of consciousness than we ordinarily use. When writing a poem, it means being open to such a level that you would never consider whether anyone would buy your poetry or even if someone would like it. If you don't create from this higher level, egotism and anxiety can enter the process, and the purest angelic help available to you may "step back" until a later time. And a composer needs to hear the music of the spheres and transcribe it out of a level of purity while not having thoughts of how wonderful the music might sound on opening night. There will be time enough for such thoughts *after* the angels have completed their inspiration.

The process I recommend is to attune your imaginative abilities to the inner peace that is available to all of us—and then to *maintain* that place of inner calm that leads to the experience of divine imagination. Then the brush may fly across the canvas, the pen move like lightning, and the sculptor's hand flash back and forth shaping the clay. And before long, the work will be completed and you will feel exhilarated and uplifted, as if you had flown for hours with the angels of God.

But if you are upset in life, take time to calm your mind and your emotions before you begin. Let go of concerns that relate to material existence. Fill your thoughts with the holiness of life, and be open to the love of the angelic realms.

As a painter, I learned a wonderful lesson in this process many years ago. I began receiving requests to paint guardian angels or specific spiritual images that were important to individuals, groups, or organizations. Sometimes the process would be completed quickly, and in other instances it might take as long as a year. There was, naturally, much work done on the inner planes with this sort of work. The reasons for delays were most often that the individuals or groups were not yet open sufficiently to receive the new impulse of light about to enter their lives through the process. They were focusing too extensively on the outer world, and they did not find sufficient time to fill their thoughts with divine subjects. I could always tell that this was the cause for the delay, because at precisely the moment when these people and groups were completely open to heaven, I could begin the physical phase of working on canvas or paper. The way was cleared to bring back to earth the images and colors of heaven that the angels wanted them to receive.

I have been aware for a long time that life is truly the greatest spiritual theater in which we choose everything from the roles of the actors to the stage setting. The angels can help us improve our creativity in developing the finest theater of life, but we have to seek the changes from out of our free will. Oftentimes, we become like actors who believe that the stage props are real, and we find ourselves attached to illusions. Then our creativity ceases to serve the heavens. The problem is not the use of matter, or our props, throughout life. The hazard is our undue attachment to matter in preponderance to inner spiritual truths.

It has been my recommendation for a long time that if we

seek to be creative or to move beyond knowledge of the angels to a place where we can work effectively *for* the angels on heaven's behalf, we need to focus on spiritual qualities that are of great importance to the angels, thus attracting their attention and help in a balanced way. We might also remember the Three Graces, as I call them, who can act as paint brush for the artist, pen for the writer, hands for the sculptor, and voice for the singer. The Graces are the spiritual creative principles of truth, beauty, and goodness. Should we align our creativity with a selfish desire to manifest only that which reflects these three qualities, we will have access to realms of heaven, which humanity can barely imagine. And, in addition, the angels will assist us in bringing to earth the most sublime through our creative process.

The world is open for us to transform if we open our souls to receive while actively creating a worthwhile vessel, or chalice, built of the highest ideals. Truly, the angels of God will respond. The first step is to enjoy new perspectives on expanding creative impulses with the loving help of your own guardian angel.

K. Martin-Kuri can be reached at Tapestry, P.O. Box 3032, Waquoit, MA 02536. Phone: 1 (800) 28-ANGEL.

An Interview With Carlos Santana

conducted by Terry Lynn Taylor

Terry Lynn Taylor: First of all, I want to thank you for all your support of my book and of the angels. My new book is about creativity and how the angels inspire us to be creative. So I am asking people who are leading creative lives to share how the angels inspire them.

Carlos Santana: Last year, when I was reading your book, I began to notice what you call angel synchronisms, funny coincidences. I was hanging out with a friend, and I asked her if she believed in angels. She got really quiet and said, "Well, I believe that there is a Supreme Power." And I said that that Supreme Power holds a chandelier, and in the light are Jesus, Krishna, and Buddha, but the crystals are the angels.

Terry: Oh, I love that.

Carlos: And she said, "Oh, okay." I wanted her to know that, because I could tell by her eyes that she is a very special person. I wanted to give her something. As Paramahansa Yogananda said, "Give us thoughts and ideas to chew all day like gum—words and thoughts that our minds can chew."

Terry: I feel like there is a lot of hope now on the planet. Do you, or do you think that things are getting really bad?

Carlos: Oh no, no, I really feel that things are bad for people who believe that without them the world cannot go on. For them, the world is ending. I think that for people who wake up in the morning and can hardly wait to do something for someone else—for them the world is just beginning. For those of us who want to complement life and serve, our world is just beginning.

Terry: That is an interesting way to look at it. On some level, that has to do with creativity, too, because if we feel creative, we have something to give, and helping others also gives us a reason to keep going. I know my own creativity seems to help when I get into a low point. I get the realization that I have got to do something creative, no matter what. What do you think creativity is? Do you think everyone is creative?

Carlos: I think that creativity comes from rousing enough enthusiasm. There is nothing more contagious. When you are enthusiastic, you can go on without food; you just go on, and people want to be around you. I also think that creativity comes from having made some kind of effort to listen to your inner voice. If you listen to your inner voice, I think that you awaken enthusiasm and imagination, which is vision. And I think that these are the two wings that we need to fly.

Terry: That's beautiful.

Carlos: Enthusiasm and imagination.

Terry: Do you know that *enthusiasm* means "filled with God"?

Carlos: Really? Wow. When I was reading your book, I was sick with an ear infection. I was really dizzy. I was wondering what was wrong with me. I had serious jet lag when I was in Germany and couldn't sleep. So I started reading your book, and I was reading about what it means to be healed, and about the dictionary definition that *to heal* means "to be whole and sound." So I said, "Whole and sound." Reading your book gave me more inner strength and inner peace–the message "You're going to be all right." Then when I found out that I had an ear infection, I was relieved to know what was causing the dizziness.

Terry: So basically that universal message came through that the angels are always trying to give us–that you are going to be okay and that the angels are looking out after you.

Carlos: Yes. They work faster than X-rays, and they can tell you immediately: "It's okay. You are all right."

Terry: Are the angels active in your life right now?

Carlos: Yeah. They add to my understanding that we are all supremely important to God, yet at the same time there are some people who belong in the category of a fuse. For example, in your house you have a fuse box. All of the lights are important in every room, but if the fuse goes, the whole house goes. So I sometimes see myself as a fuse.

Terry: So, you've created this momentum, and you have to stay with it because you are lighting up other lives.

Carlos: Right, so I am just acknowledging that that is so, and by acknowledging this I take the responsibility of thinking more with my heart than with my mind. I make it a point to say to myself, "No, think higher, from your heart." In the last two years, it has been easier for me to think, and feel, and act, and rationalize with my heart. I find myself saying "I'm sorry" less often because I don't step on people's toes. I don't have to shout to get a point across, and I wait to let others make their point. I think that people are more won over this way than when I beat them over the head with my two cents.

Terry: So you are communicating in a much higher way.

Carlos: In a much clearer way, so that people can either take it or leave it.

Terry: Does your fame get in the way of communication?

Carlos: My mom and dad are very strong in how they raised me, but I realize that ninety-nine percent is God's grace and the other one percent is personal effort. It is stupid to say "I did it my way" like the song. Can you imagine dying and going to heaven and singing that song? The angels would leave you belly up.

Terry: That is a very funny thought. So do you feel that your family is your stronghold?

Carlos: Yes, because they pray for me. I know my mom prays for me, and to tell you the truth, when I play a solo on my guitar and I am onstage, I close my eyes and I feel like I am a baby in the womb. When my mom prays for me, it is direct milk for me. So that keeps me stable, and I also know that people are flowers, music is the water, and I am the hose. So that I don't have to have the headache to make it happen.

Terry: You just are willing to do it.

Carlos: I'm just willing to get out of the way and say, "Lord if you want me to touch all those people, I will touch all those people." It's God's headache.

I know that every time I go to Paris, the audience totally goes bananas – it's like a spiritual experience for two hours, and you can just feel it. Black and white, young and old. And it just makes me realize that the music is what liberates people from within – the tone. It makes us realize that we are worth more than the sum of it all, and I think that real music happens when someone says, "I went to that concert, and it changed my life; those three notes – when you hit those notes my hair stood up and I cried and I laughed."

Terry: There has to be something to that. With music, I think hearts can really be touched and that the language of the heart happens. Can you tell when you are reaching hearts?

Carlos: Oh yeah!

Terry: It must feel really powerful.

Carlos: Actually, it sometimes feels like you are walking uphill. Once I touch the band, and I know that if I put my hand out in front and my five fingers become one, that is how it is. You get people so alive. I can tell it's happened when even the police are dancing–they forget that they are in authority. You get someone who has to be in authority dancing and–that's when I know that the spirit is overwhelming–it has taken everybody. That is what we try to do, whether it is in Germany or Japan.

Terry: You don't try; you do it. It happens!

Carlos: I have been doing this by the grace of God, since 1959, but when I played at San Quentin, I became more confident of the sound. And in Jerusalem, when the Hebrew and Palestinian people danced together at the sultan garden. At San Quentin, all the prisoners–Mexicans, black people, and white people–they all stayed. They told me that when B. B. King played there, all the whites and Hispanics left; only the black people stayed. But the warden said, "I don't know what it is about you, but they all stayed." At first they all had their arms crossed, like "Okay, *do* something for me. What are you going to do?" Then their arms went down, and they started elbowing each other. Pretty soon, they were like kids in a sandbox. So that gave me, obviously, a lot of confidence.

Terry: So you knew then that there was something more to your music than just technique—that it was reaching inside of people. That is true about your music, and you do reach across the cultures.

Carlos: That is the thing that I am waking up to, and I think a lot of people may have trouble with it, but I think most people will accept it. I believe that it is really prehistoric to think in terms of flags and borders and wallets. I know that if you and I were offered the opportunity to go on the space shuttle and go around the world for three days, we wouldn't see flags; we would see a womb, and we are all the babies. So let's get rid of this garbage of borders and flags, because it only serves to perpetuate white supremacy over other people, as far as I am concerned. I think that we need to teach people the things that Bob Marley and Martin Luther King were talking about. I went to the mountaintop, and I saw the whole picture, and there are no flags there. You know how at the beginning of the Olympics every four years everybody is dancing and crying together and the flags are just a wash of color—that is how it should be.

There is a lot to learn from the Native Americans about angels also. About certain principles. I got really involved with them and, I tell you, out of all the things I learned from Christianity and from being with a guru from 1972 to 1981 learning about Eastern philosophy, I am finding out that the cleanest and most spiritual water comes from the Native Americans. There is no contradiction there. With the Christians and the Muslims, there are contradictions—like how they treat their women. In all our meetings, whether it was Apache or Cherokee, from Canada to Brazil, they say that their women always have the last word. This was coming from an old wisdom keeper and the way he said it was clear to me that women have more of an ability to have compassion. We need to teach compassion. We all swing from the pendulum between good and bad. I think that there is another thing that we haven't tried, and that is pulling away from the pendulum. The first time I pulled away from being either good or bad was when I was in Japan and got very sick in 1981. I was so sick for three days that I had no energy to be angry or happy, and it was the first time I experienced true peace. I didn't have any energy to be good or bad. I thought, "Oh, you pull away from the good and bad pendulum, and here is compassion." I think that we haven't explored that one so much.

Terry: I agree I think it is time to go beyond good and bad, right and wrong.

Carlos: Last year, after I read your books, I got attacked by depression and frustration. I woke up one morning in Cologne, and I was just depressed. I said, "God, everything is great. My family is great, my mom and dad have been together for over fifty years. What is wrong with me?" So I heard a voice say, "Take a shower and take a walk–get lost." And I said, "Okay." So I took a long walk, and in Europe they really have a thing about flowers and gardens. All of a sudden I was in front of a beautiful garden, and I was assaulted by purples and yellows, and I heard a voice that said, "Stop and look at these flowers. The reason you are not happy is because you don't have gratitude in your heart. Flowers are put on earth to remind you what gratitude is all about. If you have gratitude, you will have happiness. If you don't, no matter who are you–Howard Hughes or Elvis Presley–you won't be happy if you don't have gratitude."

Terry: I think you are right; the two go together.

Carlos: But gratitude has to come first. I felt so embarrassed, so I said, "I'm sorry, God, and it is just a human thing." I called my mom and I said, "Now I know why they say stop and smell the flowers; it is because of gratitude." If you can enter through the world of gratitude, you will cry tears of joy and you will say, "Thank you, God, for letting me breathe and participate in this thing of yours."

The last time I heard this voice was about two or three weeks ago. Someone called me from CBS records–and I am not there anymore–and said that Julio Iglesias wanted to record one of my songs, "Europa." And he would only record it if I played on it. Now you know, I am a street guy, and we have a thing about the system. I just don't get along with the system. I'm still a hippie, and I don't go for the straight thing. So I said, "Forget it; that is not going to happen." At dinner, I mentioned this to my mom. I said, "Julio Iglesias wants to record one of my songs, but he said he would only do it if I play on it, so I said forget it." I could tell by my mother's silence, which was really loud, that this didn't go over well with her, but she didn't say anything. So I went to play tennis after eating at her house, and I threw the ball up into the air to serve and the ball never came down. All I heard was the voice, which said, "Who gave you this song?" I said, "You did." And the voice said, "Well, why don't you let me do what I want to with my song?" I said, "What do you want to do with your song?" And the voice said, "I want you to record the song with Julio, and all the money that you get from it, I want you to pledge it to the children of Tijuana. You don't need it." After this, I said, "Oh my God, okay." So I called everybody and arranged it.

To me, it is all a lesson in humility. I feel really good, because without this voice, the guitar wouldn't even stay in tune and people would go home. I have to be wise and follow the voice. It has gotten me this far.

Terry: What do you feel creative success is?

Carlos: Creative success is when you make people laugh and cry, and they accept a different reality about themselves.

Terry: Did you have a spiritual turning point with your music, or have you always been "connected" spiritually to a higher power when you are playing?

Carlos: I always knew that I had an impact on people. If they heard me playing on the street they would turn to see, and it wasn't the volume. But in 1967 and 1968, a combination of three people made me realize the universal questions. Mahalia Jackson, Martin Luther King, and John Coltrane. They were the ones who said: Who are you? What are you doing, and for whom are you going to do it? And, I said, "I am a child of God, I'm a musician, and I am going to play for God." I learned a lot of things. I learned that all of us make a promise to the Supreme Creator before we come out of the womb. We say, "Lord, thank you for the opportunity. I promise to do my best to uplift, illumine, and transform the consciousness of humanity." That is the promise we all make.

Terry: Do you think that our guardian angel knows of that promise we made when we came into the world? And do you have one or more angels keeping you on your path?

Carlos: I think there are a lot of them. It is kind of like one tree with many branches and leaves, but I think that the sap is the same. It is that sap that will help the tree go beyond forest fires and droughts and still give flowers. I tend to identify mostly with the sap, not the bark, as much as possible.

Terry: When starting a new painting, a lot of painters say they try to clear their mind of old ideas and techniques and bring something new through. Do you do that when you are starting a new album?

Carlos: Yeah. It comes in different ways. Sometimes you hear music so loud that you can't hear your wife or children talking to you. All you want to do is go in the studio and record the sound. It is kind of like when a woman is pregnant. Like giving birth–it has got to come out.

Creatively Speaking

by John Harricharan

At precisely 5:43 in the morning, exactly two minutes before my alarm clock goes off, my eyelids suddenly shoot upward. Wide awake, I reach over to shut off the backup alarm as the first misty rays of morning sun announce the debut–another fresh beginning–of yet another glorious day. It is my nature to arise early in the morning. For me, this is one of the most enjoyable parts of the day. The long night has passed, and a new day is anxious to share its promise. I find these early moments of the day to be a perfect time for my personal thoughts and reflections. For perhaps it is the only part of the day I am truly alone with myself. Someone once said that the first thing to do upon arising in the morning is to make up your bed and then make up your mind. Sometimes it's much easier to make up the bed. So, having made the bed, I shower, dress, and then go to the kitchen to enjoy my first cup of hot coffee. This is the ritual, most mornings, and I find it a comfortable and strong foundation on which to build the rest of my day.

As do most people in this decade, I lead a busy life. Yet, I always find time for the things that are important to me. We all have the same amount of time, and I have learned that it isn't the quantity of time we have but our perception of time that makes all the difference. If we learn to slow the pace of our lives a little, to indulge ourselves in "creative procrastination," we find that our minds seem sharper, that ideas appear to flow more smoothly, and that we become happier.

This is not something that one accomplishes overnight. Old habits die hard. We did not arrive where we are in one fell swoop. Ever so slowly, ever so deliberately, for reasons even we may not understand, we have created the reality we now experience. Strange as it may appear to many, our environment and our experiences are a result of our beliefs, and our beliefs are simply those ideas we hold to be true. If we do not like our current experiences, and if our experiences are a result of our beliefs, then it follows that we can change our experiences by changing our beliefs. To change our beliefs, we must first discover what they are. Therein lies the problem. Our beliefs are usually invisible, and so it takes a conscious effort to be able to uncover, examine, and change the ones that are not beneficial.

Early in the morning, as I sit at my kitchen table, fingers

curled around a steaming cup of coffee, I can look through the window and see the beginning of a brand new day. In the stillness of the morning, I seem to be more aware of who I am. I become more centered, more peaceful, more joyful. It is here that I gather all my energies together for the day that lies ahead. Ideas flow faster for me during this time. Perhaps, as I watch the mourning doves disturbing the mat of pine straw as they search for bits of breakfast, I am reminded of other times and other places and am assured, in a strange, but loving, way, that long before the mountains and the trees were, I was, and long after they are gone, I will not cease to be. For we are all part of creation and cocreators with the Creator.

Creativity itself is not relegated to any special part of the day. I feel it is a highly personal thing. For me, I am most creative in the early morning. Brad Steiger, author of over one hundred books, told me that he writes best late at night. Deepak Chopra, best-selling author of *Quantum Healing,* admitted to me that he does some of his best thinking and writing at airports and in planes. Foster Hibbard, associate of the late Dr. Napoleon Hill (author of *Think and Grow Rich*) and president of Motivation Dynamics, Inc., shared with me that he prefers the morning for his creative efforts. By listening to your inner self, you will find the best time in your daily schedule to tap into your creative fountain.

E. M. Forster, author of *Room With a View* and *Howard's End,* wrote, "In the creative state, a man is taken out of himself. He lets down, as it were, a bucket into his subconscious and draws up something which is normally beyond his reach. He mixes this thing with his normal experiences, and out of this mixture he makes a work of art." The chief enemies of creativity are the twin demons of fear and doubt. It is not fear and doubt, however, that are our undoing but the way we deal with fear and doubt. Running away or denying that we are afraid will only make our situation worse. The best way to handle fear is to face it. And how do we face it? By believing that there is a basic safety net always under us.

Change your belief system to include a friendly world instead of a threatening one and as your beliefs change, so will your world. Everything you do, everything you say, and everything you see around you are results of what you believe. When pre-Columbian peoples believed that the world was flat, it became so for them and they acted as if it were flat. When I believe that I am a victim of past injustices and that the world is an unfriendly place, it becomes so for me. When I believed that I was only a scientist and a businessman and that writing books was beyond my abilities, not a word flowed from my pen. However, when I changed that belief and realized that I had the ability and responsibility to share some of my thoughts with the world through writing, I produced the award-winning book *When You Can Walk on Water, Take the Boat,* followed by its sequel, *Morning Has Been All Night Coming.*

Personally, I know what it feels like to have my car repossessed, to watch my wife die of cancer, to see friends and family turn away from me while whispering all manner of vile rumors against me, to lose all earthly possessions, and to start over again at ground zero. If I chose to believe in the injustices of life, I certainly would have good cause. But, you see, I also know what it feels like to be featured in the same book with His Royal Highness Prince Philip of Great Britain, Paul and Linda McCartney, the Dalai Lama, and others of such caliber; to write an award-winning book; to have two beautiful, responsible children and a few loving friends. Further, I know what it feels like to sit on my back porch in the cool of the evening and watch the squirrels racing through the trees at the back of my house. These contrasts bring compassion and sensitivity to one's life.

So what is the meaning of life? Life really has no meaning. We, you and I, bring meaning to life. Does the universe owe me a living? No. I owe the universe a life. What is my purpose in life? It is to live life gloriously and to the fullest, to bring hope and joy to all those who pass my way. In short, my purpose is to make a difference, to leave this earth and its inhabitants a little better off for my having been here.

Live life joyously. Learn to trust your God and trust yourself. Practice love because it is our nature to love. Practice forgiveness not because others deserve your forgiveness but because you do. Realize that you are safe in this life and that the universe is biased on your side. Give thanks for all you have and all you hope to have and do. Live life in the present, one glorious day at a time, not spending too much time regretting the past or fearing the future. And, finally, take some time, perchance, to hear the bluebirds sing, to feel the wind in your hair, or just to witness the clouds chasing one another over distant hills.

Always Creating

by Linda Kramer

As I talked with Terry Lynn Taylor about schedules for *Creating With the Angels,* she sweetly asked me if I would like to write a piece for the book on "my ideas about creativity." Easy enough, I thought, as I agreed to do so. Why, then, was I so uneasy as I sat down to write this?

The answer soon surfaced as I allowed my mind to roam freely. Because I wanted what I said to be "good," to touch people's lives, and to contribute something to those who would take the few minutes to read what I had to say. *I wanted my audience to approve of me.*

But what if my thoughts on creativity are not profound or even very interesting? Then it struck me. Creating is something that we all do all the time. And right then I was creating a reason for not writing down my insights.

We have all tended to limit the word *creative* to describe *specific* acts of creation, such as writing, painting, dancing, or acting. But it is we who limit the word. Most of us only think of ourselves as creative if we produce a product, something that can be shown to the world and judged to have value. Mozart died a pauper, and Vincent van Gogh never sold a painting, but they and millions we've never heard of have created value. In truth, there is no escape from our creativity and the responsibility and personal power that go along with it.

We are all creating our lives at every moment with everything we think, say, believe, and choose. The difference in outcome comes from whether we are creating from our authentic self, with a feeling of ease, love, and happiness (creating in the positive), or creating from our personality self, out of a sense of obligation, fear, or the need to control (creating in the negative). Whether we admit it or not, we are all creative and creating as a necessary part of existence on the earth plane.

In my life, when I have created results that I did not want,

I often did not understand why or even that I was responsible. I have been known to blame an uncaring world or an ungrateful friend. And then I learned that you can't do, think, and say the same old thing and expect the outcome to be substantially different. Ah! A moment of truth that changed me forever.

I learned that I could interpret the thousands of stimuli that bombard my sensory system from both inside and out in such a way that I create something new. I can choose, I can have preferences, and I can allow these preferences to operate in my life from moment to moment.

So more and more I do what makes me happy, what makes me feel good. With this in mind, I create more of value. If I invite friends to dinner, I only do so if I truly want to see them. And then I take the time I need to enjoy preparing the food, choosing the music, and picking some flowers for the table. If I want to see someone and do not have that much time, then I order food sent in—with no apologies. It's the best I can do in the moment.

If a conversation begins, and I can see that I've had this conversation before and don't want to have it again, I make my excuses. And then I create something for myself that I want to do. I create a space to meditate, or water my garden, or write an article for Terry Lynn Taylor. I create something different, something that I prefer, something that makes me happy.

When my husband and I choose a book to publish, we never choose it because it will make money. We choose it because we like it, find it valuable, and want to share it with our friends in the world. In that sense, we are amateur publishers. I am told that the derivation of the word *amateur* is "one who loves." And so I am happy to be an amateur. With the help of the angels, I hope I will always be one.

Comments and a Poem by a Dancer

by Kleopatra Mishelle Leeds

Kleo sent the following contributions, beautifully handwritten on delicate paper, enclosed in an incredibly beautiful card.

It seems that all of my life has been a dance. At first and for a long time, the dance was one of pleasing and appeasing. It was full of stiff awkward missteps, anger, and uncertainty. The dance of pleasing and appeasing is constantly looking for a partner; it is compulsively and obsessively repetitious.

Recently I began to learn a new dance–the dance of joy. I embraced the dance and became joy. It was then that the steps lifted me out of codependence toward independence.

The dance of joy is surefooted and from the deep soul. It needs no partner but would easily attract the right one.

Ask Me: An Angel Song

Ask me to stem the great ocean's tide,
Ask me to halt the moon's silver ride,
Ask me to bless the blind with clear sight,
Ask me to banish all darkness from night,
Ask me to heal the wounds of the world,
Ask me to find the oyster's sweet pearl,
Ask me to live without water or air,
Ask me to cut off my breath or my hair.
But ask me not ever to cease loving you,
For that is the one thing I never could do.

On Creativity and Spirituality

by Abigail Lewis

What is creativity anyway? Our culture gives it a narrow definition that seems to be mostly limited to the arts. I love the arts. I have worked as an actress, a singer, a dancer, and a writer. In all of these creative endeavors, I've felt happiest and most alive when my work emerges from my true self.

My body is a vehicle for my true self, a vehicle that must stay in good working order to carry out its functions. But my body is not my true self, no matter how much I invest it with responsibility for my well-being. My performance, my writing, and my musical compositions are not my true self, but rather the product of my true self. So what is my true self, the ignition, the starter fluid, the context? What else is there but spirit, manifesting as talent or ability?

Creativity is available—as spirit is available—in every moment and every aspect of life, even when we sleep. I once awakened with a crystal clear, perfect fourteen-line sonnet in my awareness. It was so clear that I was sure I didn't need to pull myself into a fully wakened state to inscribe it in my journal. It was gone in the morning, of course, but, still, it had been there. Was this my creativity? Or spirit speaking through me? Are they one and the same?

I rise in the morning and make choices that shape the day. Do I take an early yoga class and center myself for the day, or do I sleep later, becoming more rested (and thus more centered) for the day? Shall I have tea first, and drink it quietly and contemplatively, or shall I wake my child and sip it by her bed as she yawns and stretches her way into the morning? Do I complain to my mate about the dirty dishes from the night before, or do I kiss him lovingly? Do I allow my daughter to eat commercial, sweetened cereal, or do I make her porridge?

I find raising my child to be a tremendous challenge to my creativity. I wonder how many of us have any real sense of what it means to be an active participant—a cocreator—in the formation of another human life. Spirit does not discriminate on the basis of race, sex, or emotional stability. But if we instill in our children an appreciation of spirit and a willingness for it to emerge, I believe we give them a tremendous advantage in life.

I hear myself talking on about spirit, and I wonder if I sound like a fanatic. There are so many interpretations of this word and this concept. If I had to align myself with any of "the world's great religions," I suppose my beliefs are closest to Buddhism. I believe there is a Big Mind that we all share and a small mind that belongs to the individual. Science now tells us that all living creatures actually share DNA, so we share not only mind but also physicality. Your exhalation is my inhalation whether or not you've brushed your teeth. We have as much in common with the Dalai Lama as we do with Saddam Hussein.

Perhaps spirit is contained in Big Mind. Or is Big Mind contained in spirit? Does it all rest in the DNA, or is the DNA just a vehicle for Big Mind? I've been asked to write about creativity and spirituality, but all I can come up with are questions.

One thing is perfectly clear. When I am feeling the most free and flowing with my creativity, I am flying. It is a creative, out-of-body experience that uses my body to communicate. Small mind and DNA step aside to allow this free flow. The greatest challenge to my creativity is to step aside and allow spirit to be my wings.

Teaching With the Angels

by Maureen Hicks

Awakening the hearts, minds, and souls of youngsters has been my mission for seventeen years. The teaching profession offers us the freedom to expand the horizons for children. Schools reflect our society. Opposition to learning abounds with the economy, social pressures, media, movies, and television—all unconcerned with the freshness in life that our children deserve. When I walk into my classroom, I know it is a magic place. It's colorful and safe.

My joy has been developing lessons that unleash the creativity in children. Creative writing has been an avenue of expression so necessary to develop within my students. I did a lesson in which I taught the children about all kinds of fairies, such as elves, pixies, leprechauns, the tooth fairy, the fairy godmother, and the countries where these fairies originated in literature. It was so much fun to then read fairy poems and stories with them. My objective was to give them the background to write their own stories about fairies. While the children read a handout that summarized the writing process, I slipped into the adjoining classroom. I quickly put on an old bridesmaid dress over my "dressed for success" suit. I stuck a crown on my head, grabbed my wand, and reentered the classroom.

My fifth graders marveled at my beauty! I picked up a basket of silver confetti from my desk and told the children that now they would be ready to write. I was going to sprinkle them with fairy dust, which would unlock their imaginations and help them to write the most enchanting stories. They wrote stories worthy of publication. The beauty of this situation was how the children responded to my awakening the child in me.

I have had an abundance of instances where the angels descended upon my classroom with miracles:

- We ordered pizzas once for the class. We didn't have nearly enough money, when all of a sudden one parent sent fifty dollars.
- I've had to handle behavior problems, and I call upon guidance from the angels to communicate effectively.
- One day I felt lonely, and a child brought me flowers.

The gifts from the angels are always creative. The more aware we become of their gifts, which are dancing all around us, the more creative we become.

Uplifted by the Angels

by Marty Noble

My paintings and drawings seek to pull the onlooker into another world, the ideal reality we are trying to achieve that is found in the integrated quality of nature and spirit.

Although my imagery is that of a romanticist, filled with

the wonder of nature and the faraway, it is also very real and strongly wants to be expressed.

As I struggle toward the light, my art does also, though it seems the art is always a few steps ahead of me and that gives me great incentive.

Though I sometimes flounder in this world, my art is created and remains apart from worldly difficulties. I find great solace in my art studio. The environment has a centering effect, reminding me that on this plane—the creative workplace—things are in order. It is like going to an altar to meditate, to a good friend to share what is important.

Since I began depicting angel imagery, I am taking new delight in my art process. There is no denying that angels are uplifting. I am uplifted and "sweetened" as I portray angels in all their caring modes of being. I have always been drawn to paint women, and painting angels is a way to express the same feminine qualities of love, devotion, and nurturing at their utmost. I am delighted to be able to contribute to the angel awareness movement.

The Spiritual Path of Creativity

by Laurel Savoie

As a child I attended Catholic schools and was taught about my guardian angel and even recited the Guardian Angel Prayer before bed every night. However, once I got older, the relationship

I once had with my angel faded away along with the strong faith and trust I once felt for the Catholic religion.

Thank God our angels never give up on us. Before I knew it, I was on my way to unfolding the truth that transcends dogma and the little bits of information organized religion reveals to us. I felt that I was being guided every step of the way.

Also while growing up, I was extremely involved in the arts—in singing, dancing, acting, and eventually songwriting. Before I wrote a song, I would meditate, ask to be inspired, and repeat positive affirmations to help the song-writing process along. This method proved to be very successful for me, and I realized how much creativity is connected to spirituality.

I found that my priorities lay not in a full-time pursuit of an acting career to appease my ego, or in being an entertainer, which can be all-encompassing, but in my spiritual evolvement and the growing relationship I shared with my husband. Besides all the support my husband and I were receiving from the spiritual kingdom, we really helped each other through this special growth process.

A real turning point along this adventurous path was learning about the Ascended Masters' teachings, my "I AM" Presence and Holy Christ Self, and a reintroduction to the angelic kingdom and guardian angels, our personal "messengers of light." Before I went to sleep at night, I started to ask my guardian angel to take me to one of the Masters' retreats, such as the Royal Teton, during sleeping hours. They say a woman's work never ends. Well, our guardian angel never sleeps and will joyfully do as we ask because service is the reason for her existence.

With my spiritual life as my main priority, I still had the opportunity to sing professionally, and when I performed I would pray beforehand and ask God to bless and inspire the audience through me. Everything was merging into one. The same was true of acting; with each thing I did, before I heard the word "action," or in TV the count off, I would silently say to myself, "I AM acting out this role and may it be perfect."

In the last couple of years, I've had a strong urge to learn more about the angels, to develop more of a rapport with them, and to have a closer relationship with these incredible "light beings." Well, ask and you shall receive. Before I knew it, I was attending a lecture given by Terry Lynn Taylor on angels. Her enthusiasm and love for the angelic kingdom was highly inspirational, and I was further along in developing a perfect union.

I was also becoming more involved in writing and, once again, with everything I wrote, I would meditate and ask for spiritual guidance. When I was asked to be on the cover of a magazine, I prepared by fasting, meditating, and prayer. The day of the photo shoot, on the fifth day of my fast, I felt clear and focused and made a special request to radiate love and light to anyone who saw the cover. While I was being photographed, I consciously allowed the light to flow in, through, and around me. I was very pleased with the results of this process.

Since then, I have actively continued a close relationship with my spirit guides and angels. I have a name for my guardian angel and feel her as a very special close friend. It's a wonderful feeling to be loved unconditionally and to know that your guardian angel has been loyal to you from day one and will continue to be with you for as long as it takes.

I have been feeling so good about reviving and creating a personal relationship with my beloved angel friends. It is up to us to create heaven on earth. Fortunately, we are not alone in this endeavor. The angels are here to assist us in every way imaginable to help carry out God's divine plan.

God, Angels, Love, and Other Wonderful Things!

by Ann Van Eps

I have been painting intensely for the last five years. I have had no formal art training, at least not in the conventional sense. All of my art training, with the exception of a couple of classes in high school, has come in a rather unusual way.

It began with an incident when I physically felt as if I had been struck by a ball of light. I had just lain down to go to sleep for the night. The room was totally dark, my eyes were closed, and I began to relax. I was thinking of how much I would like to connect up with my Oversoul. (I don't use the term Higher Self anymore, because that implies that there is a Lower Self lurking around somewhere!) I feel that as fragments of God, our connection with God, our Oversouls, angels, and anything else divine is made with love. So that night I imagined that the love I felt in my heart for my Oversoul could be likened to a beacon. Maybe even a beacon of light. Then I imagined this beautiful beacon of love/light emanating out from my heart up into the cosmos. At that point, something unexpected happened. Physically it felt like, and looked like, being hit by a ball of light. It jolted my whole body, and I felt more unconditional loving energy at that moment than at any other time in my life to that point. I felt I was floating on giant cushions of loving light.

After that night, all of my doors and windows were open to my Oversoul and my divine friends. I began having very vivid dreams of color images, and I wanted to paint my dreams, but I didn't want to take years going to art school. I was open to whatever my Oversoul was willing to have flow to me. I received detailed instructions in my dreams on how to paint and what techniques to use.

I also pull the instructions in while I paint. I have realized that in the twilight and dream state I must be an ideal student. In this state, I am very open and receptive to the point where it seems as though the information is infused into my consciousness. Later, when I am putting the information to use, it seems as though I have always known it. The flow of information is a genuine flow of love and excitement.

The dreams and visions continue. I am always behind with twenty or more paintings circling my soul waiting to be painted. In painting, I use acrylic paint, canvas, or illustration board, but the largest and main ingredient that I allow to flow into my artwork is love—lots and lots of love. Why me? Why not teach someone who already knows how to paint? I don't know the answer to that. I do know that I have *allowed* this experience. I do know that my desire to paint is very, very great. It is a part of me, just like breathing air. The desire to paint courses through me alongside life itself. Also, I *believed* my experience was possible, so it happened. I believe that experiences like mine are possible for everyone. All that is required, in my estimation, is allowing the possibility into your reality. I believe that there is a vast bank of creativity and knowledge that we can easily access if we desire.

I have realized that we feel alone when we don't express

what is inside us. When we keep thoughts to ourselves, we feel isolated. I love the world, and I strongly desire intimacy with the world. To have intimacy with humanity, I bare my soul through my paintings and share my art with the world. I keep myself accessible as an artist. I don't mind giving out my phone number, and I encourage people to communicate with me, so that I can encourage or inspire them and receive the same. I am very grateful for my gift and my existence, and for God and all the angels who have helped and guided me. I shall never take God for granted. I thank God for having the idea of me and believing in me so that I can rejoice in my existence as a part of God. I want to see God in my art. I want to paint for God. I want to be a celestial artisan!

Creativity and the Natural Cycles

by Tim Gunns

Creativity is a fundamental function of nature. The natural order of things is cyclical. Biblical reference to this phenomenon is to be found in Ecclesiastes 3:1–8, where we learn from the wise king Solomon that both history and nature move in a circle, are of a cyclical nature, an ever-revolving and recurring circle. Everything within the physical universe exists within a cycle; it is born, develops, matures, dies, and its essence is reborn. With astrology, we can study these cycles of unfoldment and learn to work with them.

Since time immemorial, humans have believed that God exists, or lives, in the heavens above, attended by a retinue of spiritual beings, angels, who oversee the various phases of cyclical evolution; thus, the sky has always been held sacred.

The earth completes one cycle, or evolution, around the sun every 365 days (creating an optical illusion of just the opposite–that the sun circles the earth) along a path through a narrow band of the heavens known as the ecliptic, or zodiac belt, allowing for the subdivision of the heavens into the twelve zodiac signs with which most people today are familiar.

The sun appears superimposed over each zodiac sign, or *sun sign,* for about a month during its (but in fact, the earth's) annual cycle. When we speak of sun signs, we are actually referring to the essential qualities inherent in a particular phase of the earth's orbit around the sun.

The "essence" of each zodiacal sun sign is embodied by certain overseeing angels, who may be employed to assist your efforts in any endeavour.

The Seasonal Cycle

The seasonal changes are at the heart of sun-sign symbolism. Indeed, astrology is based upon the seasons. All of the seasonal changes occur as the sun passes into what is termed a cardinal or initiatory sign, handing over guardianship of the season (in a kind of angelic "changing of the guard") to a particular overlighting archangel, who may be called upon to lend assistance.

We experience seasons due to a 23½° "tilt" in the earth's axis. Because of this inclination, the sun appears to travel (from our geocentric point of view) 23½° north and south of the equator during its annual cycle.

Sun-Sign Chart

Sun Sign	*Dates*	*Key Word*	*Call Upon the Angel of*	*To Inspire*
Aries	March 21–April 20	I am	Power and authority	Courage
Taurus	April 21–May 21	I have	Spiritual understanding	Abundance
Gemini	May 22–June 21	I think	Loving relationships	Responsibility
Cancer	June 22–July 23	I feel	Victory and triumph	Emotional strength
Leo	July 24–August 23	I will	Spiritual strength	Achievement
Virgo	August 24–September 23	I analyze	Discernment	Insight, acumen
Libra	September 24–October 23	I balance	Harmony and order	Self-control, poise
Scorpio	October 24–November 22	I desire	Death and rebirth	Rejuvenation
Sagittarius	November 23–December 21	I see	Patience and acceptance	Understanding
Capricorn	December 22–January 20	I use	Materiality and temptation	Success
Aquarius	January 21–February 19	I know	Service and synthesis	Unconditional love
Pisces	February 20–March 20	I believe	Imagination and liberation	Creativity, trust

Season	*Cyclical Point*	*Sun Sign*	*Overlighting Archangel*
Spring	Vernal equinox	Aries	Rafael
Summer	Summer solstice	Cancer	Uriel
Autumn	Autumnal equinox	Libra	Michael
Winter	Winter solstice	Capricorn	Gabriel

Spring, the vernal equinox, is the beginning of the natural cycle (this is in the northern hemisphere; it would be the autumnal equinox "down under"). At the vernal equinox, the sun crosses the equator, heading north. Equinox means equal day and night, or an equal amount of daytime and nighttime. From this point, the days get longer and the nights shorter.

The sun reaches its maximum northerly travel of 23½° north at the summer solstice, at a point known as the Tropic of Cancer. Solstice means a time when the sun appears to stand still in the sky, at the points of its maximum travel, referred to as the tropics. Now the days begin to "draw in" and the nights lengthen. At the autumnal equinox, when day and nighttime are equal again, the sun recrosses the equator, heading south.

The winter solstice occurs when the sun reaches its maximum southerly travel of 23½° south, and hovers over the Tropic of Capricorn, before heading north again, back toward the equator, heralding the vernal equinox, the return of spring, and the beginning of a new cycle of earthly experience.

Working With the Lunar Cycle

Angel lore concerning the lunar cycle includes the following:

- At the new moon, when we don't see its light, the angels go "inside" and get creative.
- At the full moon, the angels come out, spreading light.
- The new moon occurs when the sun and moon align in the same sign, at the same degree or zodiac point.
- Each new moon occurs in successive sun signs, that is, the next zodiacal sign in sequence (the cycle begins with Aries and ends with Pisces).
- When the new moon occurs in your sun sign, it is an especially empowered time that is supportive of your creative enterprise; that is, it can provide impetus to initiate new creative projects or beginnings. You can gain additional assistance if you also enlist the help of the angel "overlighting" the period (see the chart on p. 206).
- Between new moons (a twenty-nine and a half day cycle), the moon passes through each of the twelve sun signs or zodiacal sectors (a cycle within a cycle), spending about two and a half days in each sign. While in a particular sign, the moon absorbs and reflects the qualities and properties of that sun sign, and we may call upon the angel overlighting the particular sun-sign period, for help.

The lunar cycle comprises four quarters or phases, which correspond to the seasons:

Phase/Quarter	*Season*	*Associated With*
New Moon	Spring	New beginnings, initiation, new ideas, new growth
First Quarter	Summer	Further growth and development, adjustments

Phase/Quarter	*Season*	*Associated With*
Full Moon	Autumn	Maturity, completion, fulfillment, harvest
Last Quarter	Winter	Retreat, disintegration, reflection, preparation for rebirth

Humanity has worked successfully with these natural cycles, and the overlighting angels, down through the ages. It behooves us all to continue to do so.

For Further Reading and Reference

The Angels Within Us by John Randolph Price, published by Ballantine Books.

Jim Maynard's Pocket Astrologer by Jim Maynard, published annually by Quicksilver Prods.

Llewellyn's Moon Sign Book, published annually by Llewellyn Publications.

Watch Out for Wings

by Sally Allen

Did you ever have the motivation from within to suddenly work with clay or some medium and you never before had any artistic ability? And the end result was a masterpiece? Did you awaken in the middle of the night with a very profound statement that needed to be recorded? I have known others who have become, virtually overnight, accomplished musicians from having a dream. The "Advent of the Age of the Angels" is before us, and once again angels are reaching many people.

I believe that we are all creative. The people who never achieve are the ones who never ask and never explore. Successful creativity entails always challenging yourself and not one another. Minding the business of what others are achieving robs you of the time to find faith in your own creativity. Paying too close attention to what others are doing will not allow originality. Being competitive is not being original, and time is lost.

If you ask, the angels will show you that to be creative does not always mean being skillful in art. Loving can be creativity wrapped in a package and given with special care and devotion. Hope is carefully shown with the strength of the sun rising each morning and a breathtaking view of the mountains. Being creative is living life to the fullest with freedom.

By becoming enlightened with your guardian angel, your angel will be felt and seen not only by yourself but by others. Your creativity will flow, and your dexterity will become refined. Being creative is not based on the monetary value people seem to associate with success. Success is based on inner happiness, which can't always be seen, touched, or felt.

Many talented people from the past, such as Raffael Santi, who painted the two famous cherubs we refer to as "Raffael's angels," have continued over the centuries to bring joy, laughter, and love. Their continuity with new and aspiring artists, writers, and speakers, blesses the minds of others and helps create a healthier and more peaceful planet.

For all those who feel that creativity is too difficult or that their drawings, writings, or gifts of love are not good enough,

I assure you that somebody at sometime will need your talents. Go for it! Remember, there may be angels flying in your room; watch out for wings!

My Guru

by Allan P. Duncan

One spring day in 1983, I was sitting on a bench near the pond at Mill Creek Park. I had been trying to write some poetry, but for some reason the creative juices just weren't flowing that day and I ended up frustrated and angry. I hate to waste my time, so I wondered what I could do to make my visit worthwhile.

For several years, I had been involved in an intense spiritual search. I wanted to find the meaning of life. I wanted to find God. I wanted to become a better person and make a greater contribution to society. I had read hundreds of books on religion, philosophy, and psychology, trying to find the answers to questions that puzzled me, but I realized that all I got from these books were other people's opinions and ideas. I am a rebel at heart, and I do not accept things on blind faith. While sitting on that bench, I realized that I not only had a bad case of writer's block, I also had hit a wall on my spiritual path.

I realized that what I needed was a teacher, or guru, an enlightened master to help me along the way. South Jersey is not considered to be one of the great spiritual meccas of the world, so my work was cut out for me. The closest thing we have to a saint in Jersey is Bruce Springsteen, and I had already made my pilgrimages to the Asbury Park Boardwalk. I couldn't afford to move to India, the West Coast, or even Philadelphia, for that matter. I realized that I was stuck in South Jersey and had to make the most of it.

I remembered a Buddhist saying from my readings that said, "When the mind is ready, the teacher comes." I knew that my mind was ready as I could go no further without a teacher. I decided to resort to divine intervention, and I swear that I prayed harder that day for a teacher than I had ever prayed in my life.

When I opened my eyes, I fully expected to find before me a wise old sage wearing a long white robe, with long flowing hair and a beard. Instead, what I saw was a little girl throwing pebbles into the pond. She looked to be around seven years old. She was wearing a navy blue jumper with a white blouse and had on red and white knee socks and shiny black shoes with ankle straps and silver buckles. She had chestnut hair tied back in a pony tail that danced to and fro with her every movement.

I watched the little girl play by the pond for about five minutes. She skipped and jumped and ran around the pond, picked up some stones, and threw them as far as she could into the water. She squealed with delight when the stones hit the water and jumped up and down, clapping her hands. The smile on her face touched the core of my being. It was a smile that I will never forget, because it taught me something.

I watched the little girl flow from moment to moment in total joy, totally oblivious of the past or the future, totally oblivious of the problems of the world, just simply being. She was happy and peaceful just living in the Now, and I envied her.

I decided to lighten up a bit and take off my hair shirt.

I decided to seize more moments and have more fun. I realized that this is all there is, and I didn't want to miss any of it.

The little girl was my guru that day, and I fully believe that God sent her to me to teach me a lesson. I even believe that she might have been a little angel. I learned that gurus do not all wear white robes or have long hair and beards. I learned all this that day by directly observing the little girl in her moments of joy. She did not speak to me directly to tell me how she had achieved her joyous state. In fact, I didn't hear her say one word. I just saw her joy with my own eyes.

I also realized that not only the little girl but everything around me could be my guru. I realized that Mill Creek Park or anywhere else I happened to be was a microcosm of the universe, and that if I flowed in the moment and carefully observed nature, from somewhere within me the answers to questions that used to baffle me would come. God lives in South Jersey, just as surely as he lives in the Himalayas.

Expressing Love, Pure and Simple

by Susan Ragsdale

As human beings, our true destiny is to be angels. In this paradise called earth, we are highly evolved and have the ability to create. Life is such a blessing! In the same way that the composer is not separate from the music, the dancer not separate from the dance, and the painter not separate from the painting, God, the Creator, is not separate from his creation. Everything

I see is God, and I'm grateful to be part of it. We're not here merely to enjoy, but to *adore* all we are given. We must greatly love, worship, and honor the sacred gift of life. *I am wholly committed to serving God, and this is what it means to be an angel.*

This revelation didn't just happen. I've consciously worked for it because I've suffered and felt dissatisfied. I'm forty-one, and finally I've experienced a spiritual breakthrough. About thirteen years ago, I had some serious health problems. I became well by studying macrobiotics, which taught me how to live a natural life-style that includes regular exercise and excellent nutrition. Five years ago, I discovered Siddha Yoga and devoted myself to a spiritual master, Gurumayi Chidvilasananda. I continue to meditate, read scriptures, and chant praises to the Lord in Sanskrit. Following this path has opened my heart to love, and I have been blessed with immense gratitude.

One of the ways we can express adoration is by creating. When I paint what is beautiful to me, I honor what I see and share my vision with others. Until fairly recently, I was motivated to publish my artwork as note cards by a desire to be appreciated for my abilities. Fortunately, I no longer want this recognition. Through God's grace, I have attained humility, and I simply want to serve and be an angel.

I really enjoy painting. It comes naturally to me, and the work keeps getting better. It's a wonderful way to express adoration and joy. I want to share these feelings with as many people as I can, so I publish note cards from the paintings.

The act of giving and sending cards is a special way for us to connect with others and to communicate feelings. Essentially, it allows us to express love, pure and simple. I believe in love. God is love. With love, this world is a heavenly place.

Therefore, it is my intention to create beautiful note cards that are an *inspiring* means for sharing love. Amen.

The Story of "The Angel"

by Amy Stein

In October 1990, I was working on a deadline, the completion of a final painting for the opening of my art show on October 13 at the Olson Gallery in Santa Fe. I was experiencing intense stress and anxiety as I began the painting. I was not happy with the quality of the art for the show, and I needed this painting to be powerful. I felt that I had one shot at it, no second chance, because the opening was three days away. I started painting with my usual materials–gouache (watercolor) and watercolor paper–to create a portrait of an Indian woman who probably lived in the early 1900s. The haunting photograph showed an intense and sad young Apache woman.

Somehow, it was not going right. The application of the paint seemed too thick, muddy in places. I felt for an instant both hopeless and frustrated. Should I throw it out? Start again? There was no time. I kept on working. I briefly sketched in the oval shapes to the left and right of her head which were to be her grandparents behind her. I tried not to think, just kept on working on her face. Suddenly it seemed that this woman's face jumped off the paper, came alive, and confronted me.

It is not uncommon for me to experience, as a portrait

painter, this moment when paint becomes transformed into an alive presence, a consciousness that confronts the artist, but this was somehow different. I experienced this moment as a "jolt" of recognition, a "shock." It is an interesting feeling to have something you've painted suddenly confront you. Her expression was one of incredible love, compassion, and tenderness, with an amused half smile. I was caught off guard, and I remember gasping and moving backward, suspended in time somewhere.

I moved toward the painting again, brush still in hand, to fill in the faces of the grandparents behind the Indian woman. It was as if she looked directly at me and spoke these words: "Those are not my grandparents; those are my wings. I am an angel. We love you; everything is all right. Put down your brush; it is finished." I remember dropping my brush on the floor, my eyes welling up with tears. The painting was finished.

The painting was framed, called "The Presence," and hung at the Olson Gallery for the opening. In the weeks and months that followed, people started calling it "The Angel," the angel with the Mona Lisa smile. Two weeks after I painted it, I tried to understand what was so unique about this image. I realized that there were two distinct sides of her face that were apparently unrelated but integrated. A light side that was smiling, and a dark side that had an expression of intense sadness and tragedy. The woman unflinchingly confronts the viewer. I realized what an angel was—a soul who had experienced tragedy and sadness but continued to love. I feel that in this painting, I healed and integrated different parts of my personality with love and compassion. This angel continues to be a nourishing and healing image to me and others.

Poets and Angels: A Tour of Angel-Inspired Poetry

by Shannon Melikan

Every hour, every moment has its specific attendant spirit.
H. D., "Tribute to Angels"

If the angels are everywhere, then they are particularly abundant in poetry. In fact, they take up residence there and can be found anytime, living, playing, and reporting messages of love to us through the poem. Because poetry is mystical, between the lines that speak so boldly to our souls are doors to heaven. Here the living, moving Word shapes itself to our psyches, and God becomes intimate and absolutely personal to us.

Words, like the word itself, themselves can be reincarnations.
Norman Holmes Pearson, Foreword to *Trilogy* by H. D.

In poetry, angels often have names and identities. They speak to us clearly and impart encouragement that is forever generous in its nature. We know that we can go to a poem where a known angel resides and be quickened by a burst from the page that embraces us and endows us with the kiss of heaven. For poetry is a haven (heaven)–another world where an open, yet secret, mystical celebration waits patiently between the lines, entwined in the metaphorical language of words.

In some poems, the angels become more sparklingly simple. When the light shines on something, we notice it, and when angels highlight beauty, we understand the miracle of it. Angels shine and appear to poets for our benefit, because the poet is a scribe, talented and loving toward people, by taking the care and time to see and describe these beautiful creatures.

Rainer Maria Rilke describes angels in a magnificently expansive way in this excerpt from *The Second Elegy, Duino Elegies.* We can infer that angels can be anything they desire.

Early successes, Creation's pampered favorites.
Mountain-ranges, peaks growing red in the dawn
Of all Beginning—pollen of the flowering godhead,
joints of pure light, corridors, stairways,
thrones,
of emotion whirled into rapture, and suddenly alone
mirrors, which scoop up the beauty that has
streamed from their face
and gather it back, into themselves, entire.

The poet H.D. zooms in with utter concentration to take an intense, close look at the life form of an angel. In this excerpt, she was sitting around with two friends, writing the second part of *Trilogy*, entitled "Tribute to Angels." In this section, one friend, whom she refers to as her patron, pushes her to describe the quality of the angel she sees.

I can not invent it,
I said it was agate.

I said, it lived, it gave—
fragrance—was near enough

to explain that quality
for which there is no name;

I do not want to name it,
I want to watch its faint

heartbeat, pulsebeat
as it quivers, I do not want

to talk about it,
I want to minimize thought,

to concentrate on it
till I shrink,

dematerialize
and am drawn into it.

H.D. is mesmerized by looking at the angel, and she protests being pushed to describe it. But within her protest, she brilliantly shows us how to concentrate on angels. Within this poem are meditative instructions for the mystical experience.

The "angel onset"–the wisdom, the happening, and the influence of the angels–is the way Alfred, Lord Tennyson describes the inspired work of Milton in the poem "ALCAICS":

O mighty-mouthed inventor of harmonies,
O skilled to sing of Time or Eternity,
    God-gifted organ-voice of England,
    Milton, a name to resound for ages;
Whose Titan angels, Gabriel, Abdiel,
Starred from Jehovah in gorgeous armories,
Tower, as the deep-domed empyrean
Rings to the roar of an angel onset– . . .

And a wonderful example of what Tennyson describes as an "angel onset" is in the angelic instruction on happiness in Milton's *Paradise Lost:*

To whom thus also the angel last replied:
"This having learned, thou hast attained the
sum of wisdom; hope no higher, though all the stars
Thou knewest by name, and all the ethereal powers,
All secrets of the Deep, all Nature's works,
Or works of God in heaven, air, earth or sea,
And all the riches of this world enjoyest,
And all the rule, one empire. Only add
Deeds to thy knowledge answerable; add faith,
Add virtue, patience, temperance, add love,
By name to come called charity, the soul
Of all the rest; then wilt thou not be loth
To leave this Paradise, but shalt possess
A Paradise within thee, happier far.–

In Dante's Divine Comedy–Inferno, Purgatorio, and finally, Paradiso–his deceased love, the now angelic Beatrice, is sent from Heaven to save Dante's soul from what is described as "the dark wood of error":

Her eyes were kindled from the lamps of Heaven.
Her voice reached through me, tender, sweet, and low.
An angel's voice, a music of its own:

The Divine Comedy records the visions and experiences of Dante as he is transported through hell, purgatory, and finally paradise, where he has the ultimate vision of universal harmony:

And in the center, great wings spread apart,
more than a thousand festive angels shone,
each one distinct in radiance and in art.

Here, Beatrice is real and eternal, for she exists for us as well as for Dante and does not disappear from human awareness, but reappears later in Lewis Carroll's poem "Beatrice":

In her eyes is the living light
Of a wanderer to earth
From a far celestial height:
Summers five are all the span–
Summers five since Time began
To veil in mists of human night
A shining angel birth.

Finally because angels come and go as they see best, and it is better not to demand or expect personal appearances by them, we can always join as poets to praise them, as John Keats does here in "Spirit Here That Reignest":

Spirit here that laughest!
Spirit here that quaffest!
Spirit here that danceth!
Noble soul that pranceth!
Spirit! with thee
I join in with glee. . . .

Works Cited Bibliography

Carroll, Lewis. "Beatrice." In *The Humorous Verse of Lewis Carroll.* New York: Dover Publications, 1960.

Dante (Aligheri, Dante). *The Inferno* and *The Paradiso*. Translation by John Ciardi. Canada: A Mentor Book (a division of Penguin Books, USA, Inc., New York), 1982.

H.D. "A Tribute to Angels." In *Trilogy*. New York: New Directions, 1973.

Keats, John. "Spirit Here That Reignest." In *The Poems of John Keats*. Edited by Jack Stillinger. Cambridge, MA: Belknap Press of Harvard University Press, 1978.

Milton, John. *Paradise Lost*. Chicago: Donohue, Hennesberry & Co., n.d.

Pearson, Norman Holmes. Foreword to H.D., *Trilogy*, pp. 13–15. New York: New Directions, 1973.

Rilke, Rainer Maria. "The Second Elegy." *Duino Elegies: The Selected Poetry of Rainer Maria Rilke*. Edited and translated by Stephen Mitchell. New York: Vintage Books.

Tennyson, Alfred Lord. "ALCAICS." Cited in *The Penguin Book of English Christian Verse*, p. 241. Edited by Peter Wevi. London: Penguin Books, 1984.

What I Think Is Creative

by Jessica Marie Godfrey, age 9

What I think is creative is angels and what they wear. I think angels are creative because they help people and because they are so pretty. Angels are also creative in what they say to people.

Another thing that is creative is nature. I love every part of nature. I think nature is creative in the birds that flap their wings and the horses that run.

I also think my aunt, Terry Lynn Taylor, is very creative. She writes books.

Closing Thoughts

Make creativity a priority in your life! Make creating heaven a priority in your life! So many issues we face have an answer that we will find by expressing our own individual creative spirit. One answer I personally have received through creative inspiration concerns the importance of gratitude. I've found that if I'm not happy, the missing ingredient is gratitude. The first thing I do when I am not feeling happy is look for ways to express my gratitude. One way to do this is I simply ask the angels for a boost in gratitude, and I quickly receive it.

I have hope because I see the world getting better. I have many blessings in my life, and one special one is that I get to receive mail from people who are really making positive changes in their lives because the angels have helped renew their sense of hope. I know that there is a revolution going on in the hearts of the people; I have proof of it. The revolution hasn't quite reached all people's minds yet, so not all may understand it fully, but the revolution has begun and *that* is why the angels are so popular right now. The angels are here not to make us richer in money or worldly possessions but to make our lives richer with meaning and our hearts more alive with the energy of love. For this I am grateful.

I continue to write books for two main reasons. First, because of you, and, second, because you, your angels, and my angels inspire me to. Many people ask me the question: "How many copies of your books have you sold? How much money are they making?" That seems to be the big deal—the more books sold, the more successful or the richer I must be. Well, I don't look at success in terms of numbers and money. In my mind, the real questions are: Do my books reach people? Do they touch hearts? Am I happy that I wrote them? I can honestly answer yes to all three questions, and for that I am very *grateful*.

May the angels of light bless your soul with everlasting joy. May they dance in your mind, bringing an endless stream of noble thoughts. May your heart overflow with angelic love. And may your life continue to be an angel-blessed, creative miracle.

Acknowledgments

I am grateful to the following people for their positive influence on my life and my creativity. For this particular book, I must first go back in time and acknowledge those I remember for their positive influence on my young creative energy. I am truly grateful that they exist. Writing acknowledgments can be very autobiographical, and I say, "Why not?" Acknowledgments are also for posterity. I like the idea of acknowledgments providing a chance to be indulgent. I encourage everyone to write acknowledgments once in a while. If you are not putting them in a book, put them in your journal or somewhere special.

I guess I was a strange child by most people's standards. At least that message was conveyed to me several times by the adults and children I grew up around. However, I was very loved! And very blessed, because there were a few key people who took my oddness and helped me express it constructively. Of course, my parents and family provided the foundation. Every art project I brought home was considered a masterpiece, and any noticeable talent was allowed room to flourish. It took me a long time to fully grasp and appreciate the integrity that my parents, Gordon and Nancy Taylor, sought to instill in me. The more I understand the importance of integrity, the more in awe I am of my blessing of having these two people as parents. There are some people who naturally leave a positive and life-affirming mark wherever they go. My Aunt Dorothy was like that. I only saw her once a year, and she died too young, but every time I did see her—and also in her letters—she left me with a positive thought about myself that pulled up my self-esteem and made me think. My grandmother Dorothy Kelley also came through at important times to encourage me and let me know that ultimately everything would be okay.

Outside my family, encouragement came first from my friends and then from my art teachers. My first real art teacher was Betty Mae Anderson. When I think of her, I think of her humor, her wonderful eccentricity, the way she created a safe place to express oneself, and of course the inspiration she created through her own art. Another art teacher/artist who inspired me at a young age was Ann Lascombe. She taught me to understand the energy of nature and to see the beauty in the mountains and in the natural world that surrounds us wherever we live. She was also the mother of one of my most favorite friends, Kari, and I always felt Ann treated us more like people than like children.

Anya Fisher, my high school art teacher, taught me how to really look at what I was seeing. I am grateful to her for that gift and for her inspiring poetry and art. She was the first woman who really taught me, by her example, that being an older woman in our society is an inspiration and full of blessings instead of something full of fright and dread.

Ed Wortz has been a stabilizing influence on my life and creativity over the last eighteen years; I truly appreciate his Zen way of being and his sense of humor, which has continuously renewed my own sense of humor during crucial times.

There are many others who positively influenced my early years, and I wish I could list them all. Their light will always shine, for the light of love continues to touch hearts far and wide.

Currently, I thank my sister Kathy for her support. I thank my niece Elizabeth for her contribution—the dedication to the book—and for the joy of witnessing her grow into such a beautiful person. I thank my niece Jessica for her addition to the book, and I'm grateful to both her and my nephew Nichols for being an everlasting source of inspiration and humor. And I thank my brothers, Tim and Kevin, for being my brothers.

The Family of This Book

I acknowledge and feel immense gratitude toward the following people who helped in the birth and development of this book. Linda Kramer is the birth partner or creative midwife for this project. This book started out as a guided journal with very little writing involved. Through Linda's guidance and inspiration, it grew into what it is, which is much more than I even imagined I had in me to say. For this, and for her friendship and her contribution to the Creativity Forum, I am very grateful. Hal Kramer is the rainmaker. I am convinced that just by his very presence, magic is created around a book he publishes. Nancy Grimley Carleton is the human guardian angel of this book. She has a masterful art of editing that results in integrity, something of which she has an abundance to give. I also thank her for being there at crucial times with just the right word of encouragement for my personal needs.

Tim Gunns is this book's brother. I can always count on him to be there when I need a little extra protection and support, and his presence in my life allows me the safe room to explore and grow spiritually. I thank him for this and for his contribution, which I asked him to make with vaguely specific ideas in my mind. He was able to synthesize my request and come up with a wonderful addition.

Shannon Melikan is truly the sister of this book. So many parts of it were inspired by a conversation or a perception we would discuss, or by the idea that I have a witness. She was able to put into words many of the concepts I wanted to write about beforehand, so that I was able to allow more clarity into what I was writing at the time. I thank her, too, for the wonderful tour of angel poetry. Poetry is close to her heart, as the angels are, and I am so glad she shared some of her studies of both subjects in this book.

The Extended Book Family

I thank the following people for their contributions to the Creativity Forum and for their positive embellishment to my life: K. Martin-Kuri, for the spiritual gifts she has brought to my life, her integrity as an angelologist, her support for my work, and for writing the foreword to this book. Susan Ragsdale, for her essence of purity and love. Ann Van Eps, for her enthusiasm, love, and cheerleading for the light. Kleo Leeds, for inspiring others to dance through life in the light. Carlos Santana, for his support of my *play* with the angels and for being one of the most inspiring human beings the world will know–through his music, his humility, and his outlook on life. Marty Noble, for the beauty, grace, and kindness that come through so clearly in her art. Laurel Savoie, for the extra laughter she brings with her wherever she goes, and for the inspiring example of spiritual integrity in body, mind, and spirit that she is. Abigail Lewis, for her intelligence, which is pure and loving, for her humor and synergistic effect on my creativity ideas, and for her generosity in spirit. Sally Allen, for her humorous take on life, which has helped to keep me sane, for helping me keep the light in perspective, and for sharing so honestly her feelings about life, love, and the angels. Allan P. Duncan, for sharing his lessons in life so others will be inspired and for writing and sending just what I need at the right time. Maureen Hicks, for her dedication to the positive future of life, for her own abundant life force, and for her sense of fun. Amy Stein, for sharing her blossoming angel consciousness through her art and her life to inspire others to keep going no matter how tough it gets. John Harricharan, for so many things and for being a rainmaker in my life. So many blessings have come my way since I met him that have a direct correlation to him; truly important to me is the blessing of his friendship and the power of his pure inspirational motivation he so freely shares with the world.

Significant Others

I also want to acknowledge: Mary Beth Crain, for her friendship, her humor, and her creative life, and for being a kindred spirit. Jai Italiander, for her unending generosity, love—an example of service to God—and true friendship. Uma Ergil, for her kindness and friendship. Mick Laugs, for his comedic timing. And Anita Keeler, for her positive support. My neighbors, Marie, Oriann, Eli, Kim, Sandy, and Tors, for the added dimension they have brought to my life and so to this book. The many *Angels Can Fly* members and readers who write to me keeping my angel consciousness strong, light, and bright with hope. Fred Hansen, for the spirit of believing in oneself and one's mission in life. And, finally, Lisa Rome, for her child of life spirit and her friendship.

Book and Resource List

Books on Creativity

Cameron, Julia. *The Artist's Way.* New York: Putman, 1992.

Diaz, Adriana. *Freeing the Creative Spirit: Drawing on the Power of Art to Tap the Magic and Wisdom Within.* San Francisco: HarperCollins, 1992.

Kent, Corita, and Steward, Jan. *Learning by Heart: Teachings to Free the Creative Spirit.* New York: Bantam, 1992.

Miscellaneous Books

Fisher, Robert, *The Knight in Rusty Armor.* Hollywood, CA: Wilshire Book Company, 1990.

Parrish-Harra, Carol E. *The Book of Rituals: Personal and Planetary Transformation.* Santa Monica, CA: IBS Press, 1990.

Scheffer, Mechthild. *Bach Flower Therapy: Theory and Practice.* Rochester, Vermont: Healing Arts Press, 1988.

Angel Books and Resources

John Ronner's *Angel Book Catalog* is one of the largest sources of angel books anywhere. Includes hard-to-find books, clip art books, and cassettes. To receive a free copy of this catalogue, send a stamped (52¢ postage), long #10 envelope to Mamre Press, 107-AF South Second Ave., Murfreesboro, TN 37130. John has a new book out, *Know Your Angels: Meet One Hundred Prominent Angels From Legend and Folklore.* If you have trouble finding it, you can order it directly from him by sending $10.95 plus $1.50 shipping to the address above for Mamre Press. This great book lists many of up-to-date resources, and it is fun to read.

Maclean, Dorothy. *To Hear the Angels Sing.* Hudson, NY: Lindesfarne Press.

I highly recommend this book. It is still my top favorite of angel books. If you have trouble finding Dorothy Maclean's book *To Hear the Angels Sing,* you can order it directly from Lindisfarne Press for $10.95 and $3.50 for shipping and handling. Phone (518) 851-9155. (Visa/Mastercard accepted.) Send check or money order to Lindisfarne Press, RR 4, Box 94 A-1, Hudson, NY 12534. This is also the address for the Anthroposophic Press, so you can request their book catalogue for further angel information. Phone: (518) 851-2054.

Two books I highly recommend for deepening your relationship with the angels (which appeared on the scene after my list in *Messengers of Light* was compiled) are

Daniel, Alma; Wyllie, Timothy; and Ramer, Andrew. *Ask Your Angels.* New York: Ballentine, 1992.

Howard, Jane. *Commune With the Angels.* Virginia Beach, VA: A.R.E. Press, 1992.

Special Angel Gatherings

Power Places Tours will be featuring a sping 1994 conference on Angels and Nature Spirits in Hawaii and a future one in Ireland and England. To find out about these special events and other exciting trips they offer, contact them at: 285 Boat Canyon

Drive, Laguna Beach, CA 92651. Phone: (800) 234-TOUR (8687) outside California; inside California: (714) 494-5138

Tapestry hosts an annual weekend conference on angels, offers tapes, and an angel class workbook. Contact Tapestry at 1 (800) 28-ANGEL, P.O. Box 3032, Waquoit, MA 02536.

Aromatherapy

Throughout the book, I mention scents and aromatherapy that can assist in your play with the angels. QuietStar: The Fragrant Path® has a mail order catalogue with the best oils and supplies. QuietStar receives information from the devas about which oils to blend and for what. I have met the couple who started QuietStar and consider them kindred spirits. To receive the QuietStar mail order catalogue, write to: QuietStar, 1415 Abbot Kinney Blvd., Box 144, Venice, CA, 90291, or call 1 (800) 722-OILS (6457) for direct ordering and information.

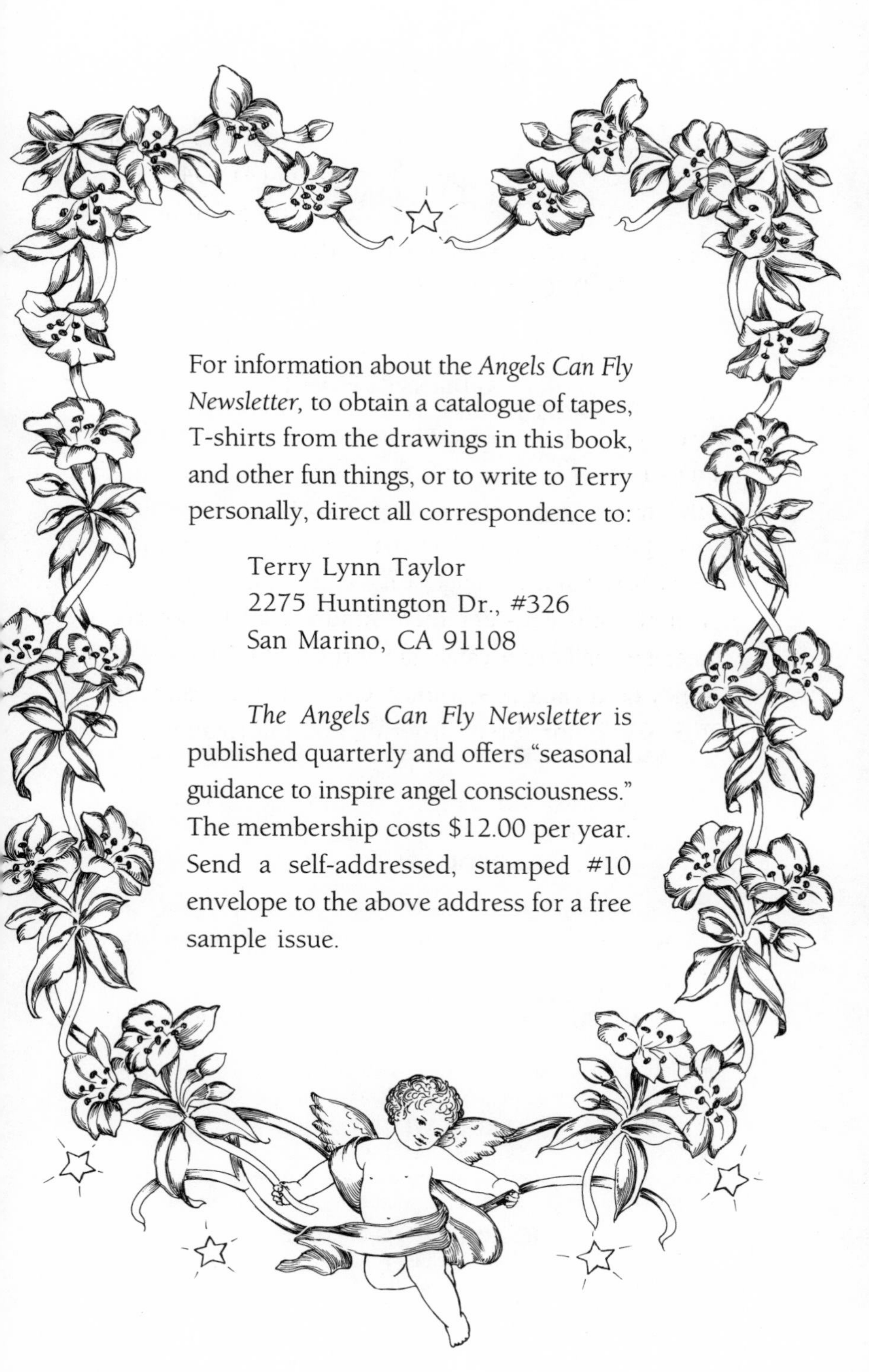

For information about the *Angels Can Fly Newsletter,* to obtain a catalogue of tapes, T-shirts from the drawings in this book, and other fun things, or to write to Terry personally, direct all correspondence to:

Terry Lynn Taylor
2275 Huntington Dr., #326
San Marino, CA 91108

The Angels Can Fly Newsletter is published quarterly and offers "seasonal guidance to inspire angel consciousness." The membership costs $12.00 per year. Send a self-addressed, stamped #10 envelope to the above address for a free sample issue.

COMPATIBLE BOOKS

FROM H J KRAMER INC

**MESSENGERS OF LIGHT:
THE ANGELS' GUIDE TO SPIRITUAL GROWTH**
by Terry Lynn Taylor
At last, a practical way to connect with the angels and to bring heaven into your life!

**GUARDIANS OF HOPE:
THE ANGELS' GUIDE TO PERSONAL GROWTH**
by Terry Lynn Taylor
GUARDIANS OF HOPE *brings the angels down to earth with over sixty angel practices.*

**ANSWERS FROM THE ANGELS:
A BOOK OF ANGEL LETTERS**
by Terry Lynn Taylor
Terry shares the letters she has received from people all over the world that tell of their experiences with angels.

WAY OF THE PEACEFUL WARRIOR
by Dan Millman
A tale of transformation and adventure . . . a worldwide best-seller.

SACRED JOURNEY OF THE PEACEFUL WARRIOR
by Dan Millman
"After you've read SACRED JOURNEY, *you will know what possibilities await you."*—WHOLE LIFE TIMES

NO ORDINARY MOMENTS
by Dan Millman
Based on the premise that we can change our world by changing ourselves, this book shares an approach to life that turns obstacles into opportunities, and experiences into wisdom.

**THE LIFE YOU WERE BORN TO LIVE:
A GUIDE TO FINDING YOUR LIFE PURPOSE**
by Dan Millman
A modern method based on ancient wisdom that can help you find new meaning, purpose, and direction in your life.

TALKING WITH NATURE
by Michael J. Roads
"From Australia comes a major new writer . . . a magnificent book!"
—RICHARD BACH, Author, *Jonathan Livingston Seagull*

JOURNEY INTO NATURE
by Michael J. Roads
"If you only read one book this year, make that book JOURNEY INTO NATURE."—*FRIEND'S REVIEW*

COMPATIBLE BOOKS

FROM H J KRAMER INC

THE EARTH LIFE SERIES
by Sanaya Roman
A course in learning to live with joy, sense energy, and grow spiritually.

LIVING WITH JOY, BOOK I
"I like this book because it describes the way I feel about so many things."—VIRGINIA SATIR

PERSONAL POWER THROUGH AWARENESS: A GUIDEBOOK FOR SENSITIVE PEOPLE, BOOK II
"Every sentence contains a pearl. . . ."—LILIAS FOLAN

SPIRITUAL GROWTH: BEING YOUR HIGHER SELF, BOOK III
Orin teaches how to reach upward to align with the higher energies of the universe, look inward to expand awareness, and move outward in world service.

An Orin/DaBen Book
CREATING MONEY
by Sanaya Roman and Duane Packer, Ph.D.
This best-selling book teaches advanced manifesting techniques.

BRIDGE OF LIGHT
by LaUna Huffines
Tools of light for spiritual transformation—a spiritual classic.

SON-RISE: THE MIRACLE CONTINUES
by Barry Neil Kaufman
The inspiring true story of one family's triumph over helplessness that started a revolution of love for autistic and other special children.

UNDERSTAND YOUR DREAMS
by Alice Anne Parker
A practical book that offers the reader the key to dream interpretation.

THE WIZDOM WITHIN
by Susan Jean and Dr. Irving Oyle
"Fascinating! Illuminating . . . Reading this book can be hazardous to your preconceptions."
—WILLIS HARMON, President, Institute of Noetic Sciences